# THE REV. LEGH RICHMOND'S
# LETTERS AND COUNSELS TO HIS CHILDREN

# The
# Rev. Legh Richmond's Letters and Counsels to His Children

*Selected from
His Memoir and "Domestic Portraiture"
with an Account of the Closing Scene of His
Life Written by His Daughter
Fanny Richmond*

BY

## REV. LEGH RICHMOND

CURIOSMITH
MINNEAPOLIS

Published by Curiosmith.
Minneapolis, Minnesota.
Internet: curiosmith.com.

Previously published by the AMERICAN TRACT SOCIETY in 1848.

Footnotes marked "original footnote" are footnotes from the original text, all other footnotes have been added to this edition by the publisher.

ISBN  9781941281796

# CONTENTS

—◦◦○◦◦—

# INTRODUCTION

The Rev. Legh Richmond is extensively known to the Christian community, as the author of those beautiful narratives which it has pleased God to bless to the conversion of so many souls: "The Dairyman's Daughter," "Little Jane, or the Young Cottager," and "The African Servant." He holds a conspicuous place among the evangelical clergy of the established church in England, who have adorned the present century.

His ministerial career commenced at Brading, in the Isle of Wight, in 1797, whence he removed to Turvey, Bedfordshire, England, in 1805. Here he continued to labor with untiring zeal, and earnest devotion, for the good of souls, till the period of his death, May 8, 1827.

But it was not merely in public life, and in the exercise of his professional duties, that his character shone with unwonted brilliancy, and won for him that rich meed of undying affection which attaches to his memory. It was at home, in the bosom of his own family, as the guardian and companion of his children, that all that was most "pure" and "lovely," and "of good report," all that was most gentle and winning in the qualities of his mind and heart, developed itself. If, as a minister of Christ, he was a "lively stone" in God's "spiritual house," at his own fireside he was burnished gold, reflecting the image, and bearing the impress of the great Refiner.

The very deep and active interest which he took in the missionary and other benevolent institutions, and the acceptableness and success of his eloquent sermons and appeals in their behalf, led to his performing several tours in various parts of England and Scotland, as the advocate of those institutions; but for which tours, a number of these beautiful letters to his children would probably not have been written. His journey in Scotland with his son Wilberforce, whose health had declined, also occasioned letters to his children remaining at home; and even under his own roof he occasionally wrote letters to his children, as a happy means of promoting their temporal and eternal benefit. These letters, selected from his memoir and the "Domestic Portraiture," and now first issued as a separate volume, bear ample testimony to the loveliness of his domestic character; and we trust they will interest and benefit the youth of our land, to whom, "he being dead, yet speaketh."

The letter from his daughter, containing the particulars of her father's last days, which is annexed to these letters, beautifully portrays the tenderness and deep veneration with which he was regarded by his children. Truly "the memory of the just is precious," and "the righteous shall be in everlasting remembrance."

## Chapter 1

LETTERS TO HIS TWO ELDEST DAUGHTERS—COUNSELS TO
THE SAME—LETTERS TO THE SAME—LETTER TO HIS ELDEST
SON—MEDITATION ON THE WONDERS OF THE KALEIDOSCOPE

*To his second daughter, Fanny.*

OCTOBER, 1815

MY DEAR CHILD—This may probably reach you on your
birthday. It is a day which should remind you of the importance of time, and the swift approach of eternity. It
bids you remember your Creator in the days of your youth. But
have you ever done so aright? Have you seen yourself a sinner, and
gone to the blood of Christ for pardon? Forms and notions never
yet saved a soul; and have you, indeed, ever gone further than forms
and notions? My child, be in earnest; it is no trifle whether you
have real grace or not: it is everything to ascertain this point, and to
act upon it. Do you feel a burden of sin for daily offenses? do you
repent? do you pray from the heart? Suppose God were to see good
to bring you to a bed of death, where are your evidences that you are
really his child? Think in how many ways you have offended him
in thought, word, and deed. What but a Saviour's blood can wipe
the guilt away?

It is full time, my dear Fanny, that you show a decision of character, in that humble yet determined separation of life, which distinguishes a common—alas, too common—*nominally* Christian
child, from a child that believes in Christ, loves God, and is taught
by the Holy Spirit.

Secret, free prayer, is a great testimony that a work of grace is begun. But do you thus pray? Have you found out the sins into which you are the most liable to fall, and most easily tempted to commit? These are your bosom foes, and must be resisted in a different strength from any which you naturally possess. That strength is only to be obtained in Christ, and by *believing* in *him*, and *him* alone. Grace, free-grace, reigns in every step of the Christian progress. Do you ever feel these things as a matter of uneasiness, or desire, or hope, or fear? It will not satisfy me, and I hope it will not satisfy you, that you have had so many advantages of a Christian education, unless you prove to yourself and me, that there is a work of the Spirit in your heart. What a delightful display the Lord gave us of his goodness and power, when that dear and beloved woman, *your* mother and *my* wife—it is my highest *earthly* privilege to call her so—lay, as we thought, on the bed of death. You cannot have forgotten it; no one that saw it ever could. But that day was a warning and a consolation for us: oh, may we use it as both. But do not deceive yourself: mere natural feelings and meltings of heart are not enough. Sin, sin is the great cause of sorrow; and *therefore* must you weep. Carry sin to Jesus; he will hide it for ever from his Father's sight. Angels rejoice when children weep for sin.

Read "Little Jane." Two Sunday-scholars at Manchester have been converted to God this summer, by reading it: and must my *own dear* child heed it not? I trust not. Pray, dear Fanny, for faith and love to the Saviour. Happy shall I be to hear from yourself— when it does indeed come from your heart—either by letter or word of mouth, that you feel a true concern for your never-dying soul. And so may God give you many happy years, if it so please him. If not, may he take you, as a pardoned sinner, to himself, in his own time. Love to my dear H.

From her, and your truly affectionate

FATHER

Tell H., that I write every word of this for her, as well as for you.

*To the same.*

KESWICK, OCT. 16, 1815

MY DEAR DAUGHTER—The exquisite beauty and sublimity of this country almost makes a pen move of itself. Never did I pass so beautiful a day as this at the lakes. I shall sing the praises of October, as the loveliest of months. This morning, at six o'clock, I was walking on the banks of Winandermere, to catch a sunrise. I had every thing I could wish, and observed the progress of day with delight. The mysterious rolling of clouds across the hills announced the first influence of the sun. Tints the most beauteous skirted the eastern clouds; those on the west caught them as by sympathy. Various patches of mountains soon gleamed with the reflection of the yet unseen luminary; and such innumerable vicissitudes of light and shade, and *claro obscuro*,[1] filled the scene as no tongue can describe. The lake, in all its length of thirteen miles, lay beneath me, with its thirty islands. I heard the early lowing of the cows, the bleating of the sheep, the neighing of the horses, the twittering of the birds, the rustling of the breeze, and rippling of the water, and dashing of the oar, in a gentle land of harmony. The sun advanced, and threw a blaze of magnificent luster over this paradisaical landscape. I soon crossed over the lake, and passed through rich scenes of wonder and loveliness. I saw Coniston and Grasmere lakes, under circumstances of peculiar advantage. Clusters of mountains and lesser hills, clothed with crags, brown fern, red lichens, green grass, purple heath, bushes, barren gulleys, cascades, wild streaks, rolling mists, bright sunshine, etc., presented incessant variety. Hill towered above hill, Alpine peaks reared their heads, groves filled the valleys, and cottages were sprinkled in wild profusion.

I dined at a little romantic inn at the foot of the mountain Helvellyn. The lake of Leatheswater extended its four miles' length close by. My parlor window faced the great hill; a mountain stream fell from a great height, tumbling with a murmuring sound down

1 Claro obscuro—The art or practice of so arranging the light and dark parts as to produce a harmonious effect. *(1913 Webster's Dictionary)*

into the vale. Something dimmed the pane of glass through which I viewed it. On inspection, I found the following lines, written with a diamond:

> Flow, mountain streamlet, swiftly flow,
> And fertilize the vale below—
> Sweet emblem of that gracious love
> Which pours down blessings from above:
> The stream of mercy, Lord, is thine—
> The lowly heart that feels it, mine.

On another pane was written,

> Forget not, mortal traveller, thou must die;
> Before thy journey's end, ask, 'Where am I?'

And once more,

> These lovely scenes before mine eyes
> Form a terrestrial Paradise.
> But *this* shall quickly pass away:
> Then seek one in eternal day.

Thence I advanced to Keswick. Before me stood the giants of the scenery—Skiddaw and Saddleback—in sublime beauty, not to be expressed. Their length, their breadth, their height, their wildness, their roughness, their smoothness, their surface, their profile, their *tout ensemble*,[1] most grand, most interesting. At length, the lakes of Derwentwater and Bassenthwaites burst upon the eye with all the charm that painters and poets love, and which Christians know how to love far better than either. The scene from a hill, a mile on the road from Keswick, so much exceeds the powers of my pen to describe, that I can only say, "How amiable are thy tabernacles, O Lord,"[2] the Creator.

I watched the moon decline on the lake, and then studied the whole scene by the finest starlight I ever beheld. Mars is now in

---

1 Tout ensemble—the general effect of a work as a whole. *(1913 Webster's Dictionary)*
2 Psalm 84:1.

the east, like Jupiter; yea, bright as a moon. The Great Bear hangs pendant exactly over Skiddaw, and Mars rises triumphantly over the summit of Saddleback; the galaxy sweeps over the hemisphere, white as milk, and clear as moonlight. All is solemn, silent, peaceful. I write you this faint breathing of expression. Could you copy these scenes, I should be proud of your company here; I trust some day you will.

This morning, as I stood on an eminence, looking down on the exquisitely-lovely lake of Grasmere, environed by its amphi-theater of mountains, a momentary shower produced a rainbow; it extended from hill to hill, over the valley, and seemed like a bridge for angels to pass over from one district of paradise to another:

> And as they *pass*, let angels sing
> The wonders of creation's King;
> And while they tune their harps to praise,
> I'd gladly catch their solemn lays;
> Unite with theirs my feeble tongue,
> And give to gratitude my song.

The following letter to his eldest daughter, Mary, is without date.

My dear Mary—I leave you, in much love, a few fatherly hints.

1. Be constant in private prayer.

2. Be wise in the choice of books; shun *every thing* of the romance and novel kind; and even in poetry, keep to what is useful and instructive, as well as pleasant.

3. In company, show that the principles of your father's house and ministry are your rule of conduct, and your real delight. Be consistent: cheerful, but not light; conversable, but not trifling.

4. Keep ever in view, that you are supporting my character and credit, as well as your own.

5. Show a marked preference to such conversation, remarks, persons, discussions, and occupations, as may tend to essential good.

6. Always think before you speak; say and do, neither hastily nor unadvisedly.

7. If any proposal is ever made to you, in which you hesitate how to act, first say to yourself, how would God have me to act? Secondly, what would my parents have me to do, if they were here to advise me?

8. Never lose sight of this: that the more public my name, character, and ministry are become, the more eyes and ears are turned to my children's conduct; they are expected, in knowledge and circumspection, in religion and morals, in opinions and habits, to show where they have been educated; and to adorn, not only their Christian profession, but their parents' principles.

9. In music, prefer serious to light compositions; and in vocal, keep close to sacred words.

10. Pray much for

Your affectionate father,

Legh Richmond

P. S.—I send you the following application of a sermon, from Ephesians 5:15, 16.

## ON CIRCUMSPECTION OF WALK, REDEMPTION OF TIME, AND GENERAL TRANSPARENCY OF CHARACTER

1. Adhere most scrupulously to truth; and labor to preserve the strictest integrity, simplicity, and sincerity.

2. Engage in no pursuit in which you cannot look up unto God, and say, "Bless me in this, O my Father."

3. Strive to be as kind, forbearing, and forgiving, as you can, both to friends and foes.

4. Never speak evil of any one, on any pretence whatever.

5. Strive to recommend religion by the courtesy, civility, and condescending character of your conduct.

6. Watch against irritation, positiveness, unkind speaking, and anger: study and promote love.

7. Mortify lusts, sensuality, and sloth.

8. Never allow others to speak well of you; nor especially, yourself to say or think any thing of yourself but as poorly done. Keep down

*pride;* let it not be indulged for a moment, and watch against it.

9. Shut out evil imaginations, and angry thoughts.

10. Let it be your *sole* business here to prepare for eternity. Consider every moment of time in that view.

11. Remember, that you have to contend with a legion of devils, a heart full of deceit and iniquity, and a world at enmity with God.

12. Pray that you may ever rejoice in the advancement of Christ's kingdom, and the salvation of sinners; and labor in every way to promote these objects.

Prayer is the only weapon which can subdue, your corruptions, and keep your evidences bright. Cultivate prayer.

We add another of these edifying testimonies of paternal solicitude and love.

TO MY DAUGHTERS—With a heart full of affection, I sit down to express a few sentiments and intimations of my wishes, as connected with your conduct, in the course of any journey or absence from home. I wish each of you to preserve a copy of it, my dear children, and often look at it; take it with you when from home, and keep it safe when at home.

Independently of my anxious wishes for your secret, spiritual welfare, I have much to feel on my own account, in point of credit and character, as connected with your deportment, in every house and company into which I may introduce you. I have not a doubt of your general affectionate wish to speak and act right; but inexperience, youth, thoughtlessness, and want of more acquaintance with the world carnal and the world religious, may easily occasion inconsistencies and errors which might be injurious to your own, as well as to my comfort and credit. Accept, therefore, a father's blessings and prayers, with a father's chapter of admonitions and explanations.

You are not unaware that my name and character have acquired much publicity; that I avowedly belong to a class of Christian ministers who profess, for Christ's and their souls' sakes, to be separate from the world—to maintain purer and more distinct views of the Scripture doctrine—and to be willing to spend and be spent in behalf of the truth as it is in Jesus. I am, therefore, supposed not only to maintain a consistent separation from the follies and vices of the world, its pomps and vanities, but to aim at so ruling and guiding my household, that my principles may shine forth in their conduct. Any want of correctness, consistency, faithfulness, and propriety in them, will always attach a mixture of censure, surprise, and concern, as it regards me. The friends of religion will grieve, and those who are otherwise will rejoice, if you could be drawn into compliances, and expressions of sentiment, at variance with your father's: always, therefore, keep in remembrance, whether you are in company with decidedly religious and consistent Christians, or with those who are only partially so, or with those who are unhappily not so at all, that you have not only your own peace of conscience to maintain, but the estimation and honor of your parent also.

Many temptations will occur, to induce you to yield and conform to habits and principles the very reverse of those which you hear me supporting, both in the pulpit and the parlor. Be not ashamed of firmly, though modestly, in such cases, resisting them. State what mine and your principles are, and heed not the momentary unpleasantness of appearing singular, when conscience and duty require it. You may easily say, "My father does not approve of such and such things, neither can I." No person whose estimation is worth having, will think the worse of you for such instances of mild but decisive firmness; and without it, I should be disgraced.

All descriptions of public amusements, novels, popular amorous poems, plays, songs, vanities, and finery, and all the sad tribe of poisonous and dangerous pursuits, should be regulated by this principle; and O, that your own simplicity and love to Christ may never give way to one sad influence of false sentiments, even amongst those whom, on other accounts, we may esteem and regard. The half-religious are often more dangerous than those who are less so, because we are more on our guard in the latter case than the former.

The great number of instances in which I have seen the young people of religious families deeply injured in their spirits and habits, by much visiting with persons of different views and customs from those of their own household, has made me, I confess, from pure motives of conscience and prudence, very averse to much of that sort of visiting in my own children's case, which I know to have been productive of bad consequences in others. And the difficulty of drawing the line has always appeared very great with my numerous friends and acquaintance. Still, I wish to make you happy in every reasonable way; and I am glad when I can give you the advantage of new scenes and company, when it is of the right kind. But as, in my journeys, extensive intercourse takes place, a great variety of characters will fall in your way; and I wish, for all your sakes, that you may be provided with sober, discreet, and religious cautions, that the natural ardor of youth may not lead you into unbecoming or sinful compliances. I know many families, and you know a few, where, perhaps, the parents are religious, but their young people are very imperfectly, if at all so; in such cases you may, from equality of age, be thrown much more into the light, frivolous, and objectionable conversation of the younger, than the more useful communications of the elders of the family. Here, often, there is danger; ever prefer and choose those, of whatever age, in whom you think you discover a holy, serious, benevolent, consistent way of acting and speaking.

A young professor of religion has not, in most instances, so difficult a task to sustain, when in conversation with those of a decidedly religious deportment, as with worldly persons, and those who can scarcely be ranked as consistently serious, although often to be met with in religious parties. If, however, your conscience be correct, you will see more and more the duty of acting and speaking aright, and you must ever pray for grace to direct and govern you. Difficulties and dangers of this kind greatly multiply, when those who, from relationship and family regard stand very near to natural love and affection, are nevertheless, in great measure, strangers to the power of true religion, and therefore mingle with the world wholly, pursue its pleasures, and support its customs. I entreat you to be much on your guard in all such cases. Decays in religious feeling and conduct continually arise from this source, and endanger the temporal, spiritual, and eternal welfare of many a hopeful family.

I am frequently placed in situations myself, where I find it very difficult to satisfy my conscience that I am doing right, amongst people and families where real religion has little or no part in their ways and conversation. In trying to be kind, attentive, and too compliant, perhaps, to *their* habits, I feel that I am in great danger of strengthening them in evil, and always of injuring my own consistency as a Christian.

I will now add some remarks, placed under select heads, which may make them more conspicuous, and better remembered: and may God render them useful to you. Keep them constantly with you, and let them be always read over at least once a week.

## AMUSEMENTS

Plays, balls, public concerts, cards, private dances, etc., etc.

Serious, consistent Christians must resist these things, because the dangerous spirit of the world and the flesh is in them all. . . . To be conformed to these seductive and more than frivolous scenes, is to be conformed to this world, and opposed to the character and precepts of Christ. They who see no harm in these things, are spiritually blind; and they who will not hear admonition against them, are spiritually deaf. Shun, my dear girls, the pleasures of sin, and seek those which are at God's right hand for evermore. You *cannot* love both.

Blessed be God, you have been kept far from those who make such recreations their idols to wean their hearts from God. Never, in any conversation, speak lightly or triflingly of these subjects, as if you had not imbibed proper sentiments concerning them. Ever preserve the consistency of your parental house and principles.

## BOOKS

Characters are speedily discerned by their choice of books. Novels in prose I need not now forbid; ignorant as you are of their bad tendency by experience, you, I am persuaded, trust me on that head, and will never sacrifice time, affection, or attention to them. But beware of novels in *verse*. Poets are more dangerous than prose writers, when their principles are bad. Were Lord B—— no better poet than he is a man, he might have done little harm; but when a bad man is a good poet, and makes his good poetry the vehicle of his bad sentiments, he does mischief by wholesale. Do not be ashamed of having never read the fashionable poem of the day. A Christian has no time, and should have no inclination, for any reading that has no real tendency to improve the heart. The finest rule I ever met with, in regard to the choice of books, is this: "Books are good or bad in their effects, as they make us relish the word of God, the *more* or the *less*, after we have read them." There are too many valuable books on a variety of subjects, which ought to be read, to allow of time to be dedicated to unworthy and useless ones.

## MUSIC

Shun all the wretched folly and corruption of light, silly, and amorous songs, on the same principle that you would shun books of the same nature. Sacred music is the true refuge of the Christian musician. I wish your ears, your hearts, and your tongues, were oftener tuned to such melodies. The playhouse, the opera, and the concert-room, have deluged the world with the abuses of the heavenly art of music. Music was designed to lead the soul to heaven, but the corruption of man has greatly perverted the merciful intention. Do not you belong to such perverters, nor seem to take pleasure in those who do.

## DRESS

Aim at great neatness and simplicity. Shun finery and show. Be not in haste to follow new fashions.

Remember, that with regard to dress, Christians ought to be decidedly plainer, and less showy, than the people of the world. I wish it to be said of the females of my house, "With what evident and becoming simplicity are the daughters of Simplex[1] attired." I refer you to my last letter on that subject.

Be cheerful, but not gigglers.

Be serious, but not dull.

Be communicative, but not forward.

Be kind, but not servile.

In every company, support your own and your father's principles by cautious consistency.

Beware of silly, thoughtless speeches: although you may forget them, others will not.

Remember, God's eye is in every place, and his ear in every company.

Beware of levity and familiarity with young men; a modest reserve, without affectation, is the only safe path: grace is needful here; ask for it; you know where.

### JOURNEYINGS

Cultivate knowledge as you travel.

History, antiquities—in cities, towns, churches, castles, ruins, etc.

Natural history—in plants, earths, stones, minerals, animals, etc.

Picturesque taste—in landscape scenery and all its boundless combinations.

Cultivate good-humored contentment, in all the little inconveniences incident to inns, roads, weather, etc.

Cultivate a deep and grateful sense of the power, wisdom, and goodness of God, in creation and providence, as successively presented to your notice from place to place.

Keep diaries and memoranda of daily events, places, persons,

---

1 Mr. Richmond's signature in "The Christian Guardian." *(Original footnote)*

objects, conversations, sermons, public meetings, beauties, wonders, and mercies, as you travel. Be minute and faithful.

Ask many questions of such as can afford useful information as to what you see.

Write your diary daily; delays are very prejudicial. You owe a diary to yourself, to your friends left at home, and to your father, who gives you the pleasure and profit of the journey.

## PRAYER

Strive to preserve a praying mind through the day; not only at the usual and stated periods, but everywhere, and at all times, and in all companies. This is your best preservative against error, weakness, and sin.

Always remember that you are in the midst of temptations, and, never more so than when most pleased with outward objects and intercourse.

Pray and watch; for if the spirit be willing, yet the flesh is deplorably weak.

## RELIGION

Keep ever in mind that, for your own sake and for my sake, you have a religious profession to sustain; and this both in serious and worldly company. Be firm and consistent in them both. Many eyes and ears are open to observe what my children say and do, and will be wherever we go. Pray to be preserved from errors, follies, and offenses, which bring an evil name upon the ways of God. You may sometimes hear ridicule, prejudice, and censure assail the friends of true religion; it ever was, and will be so: but "blessed are they which are persecuted for righteousness' sake, for theirs is the kingdom of heaven."[1] Be not ashamed of Christ here, and he will not be ashamed of you hereafter.

Court and encourage serious conversation with those who are truly serious and conversable; and do not go into valuable company

---

1 Matthew 5:10.

without endeavoring to improve by the intercourse permitted to you. Nothing is more unbecoming, than that, while one part of a company is engaged in profitable and interesting conversation, another part should be trifling, giggling, and talking comparative nonsense to each other.

Ever show the interest which you take in the subject of schools for the poor, the distribution of Tracts, the Bible and Missionary Societies, and all those important topics which so deeply occupy the people of God: and when you can find a congenial friend, talk of heaven and eternity, and your soul, and your Saviour. This will be as a shield to your head and your heart.

## ESTIMATE OF CHARACTERS

Look first for grace. Do not disesteem good people on account of their foibles or deficiencies in matters of little importance. Gold unpolished is far more valuable than the brightest brass. Never form unfavorable opinions of religious people hastily: "Charity hopeth all things." Prize those families where you find constant family prayer; and suspect evil and danger, where it is avowedly unknown and unpracticed. Always remember the astonishing difference between the true followers of Jesus and the yet unconverted world, and prize them accordingly, whatever be their rank in society.

Gentility and piety form a happy union: but poverty and piety are quite as acceptable in the eyes of God—and so they ought to be in ours. Not only are the poor far more in actual number than the rich, but experience proves that the proportionate number of the truly serious amongst the poor is much greater than the corresponding proportion of numbers amongst the rich. Take one thousand poor and one hundred rich; you will probably find ten of the latter serious, but two hundred of the former shall be so at the same time.

Beware of the critical hearing of sermons preached by good men. It is an awful thing to be occupied in balancing the merits of a preacher, instead of the demerits of yourself. Consider every opportunity of hearing as a message sent you from heaven. For all the sermons you have heard, you will have to render an account at the last day.

## PARENTS

Seek to make them happy in *you*.

If you perceive that any thing in your ways makes them otherwise, you ought to have no peace until you have corrected it; and if you find yourself indifferent or insensible to their will and wishes, depend upon it yours is a carnal, disobedient, ungrateful heart. If you love them, keep their commandments; otherwise love is a mere word in the mouth, or a notion in the fancy, but not a ruling principle in the heart. They know much of the world, you very little; trust them, therefore, when they differ from you, and refuse compliance with your desires; they watch over you for God, and are entitled to great deference and cheerful obedience. You may easily shorten the lives of affectionate and conscientious parents, by misconduct, bad tempers, and alienation from their injunctions. Let not this sin be laid to your charge.

I shall add no more at present, than that I am

Your affectionate father,

L. RICHMOND

The two following are without dates.

*To his daughter Fanny.*

. . . We are going on quietly at home. Little K——, by a sudden determination, is gone into Norfolk. My love and respect for your dear, most dear mother, has prevailed to gain my consent; otherwise I much prefer a mother's and elder sister's roof, for female education, to any school. But I leave this affair in God's hands, and hope he will overrule it for the best. I have long thought, that though a good school is better than a bad home, a good home is the best of schools. Children are, for the most part, educated in temper and habits of all kinds, not by governesses, but by companions; and here all is contingency. But so much of my own happiness consists in making your dear mamma happy, that I waive my objection to a temporary alienation from, the parental roof, and pray God it may not injure K——'s spiritual welfare. Some may think I am too fond of seeing my children around me; if it be a weakness, I must plead guilty to it: from their infancy I have looked forward, as far as providential circumstances would permit, to find comfort, support, and companionship in my children. My middle, and if spared, my old age, may much require it; and if my life be short, can any wonder that I should like to see and know much of them while I remain in this world? It has ever been my heart's desire and prayer to give them a useful, happy, exemplary home; were I to fail here, life would indeed become a blank to me. I would strive "to roll the troublous trial on God," but I should deeply mourn in secret. Sons must in due season go forth into a wanton and wicked world to seek their bread; but daughters, while unmarried, are better calculated to become comforters and companions to their parents, as they go down to the vale of years. . . .

Your affectionate father,

L. R.

*To the same.*

As I have journeyed along, I have often wished I had the pencil of a ready draughtsman, that I might bring home a bundle of sketches of landscapes, to revive recollections and render natural scenery permanent to the imagination. When I find that this cannot be, I next wish that one or more of my dear children might acquire a talent of this kind, and be a sort of right hand to fulfil my wishes in that way. Perhaps some day you will be that right hand to me. Loving landscape scenery as I do, my grand object is to see God in it; to trace him in every part of his works; to acknowledge his goodness in them, and to collect arguments from them to endear the character of Christ, "by whom," the Scripture says, "all things were made, and without whom was not any thing made that was made."[1] To this end I wish drawing to be cultivated. I mourn over pride and vanity,

---

1 John 1:3.

and if accomplishments are only acquired to gratify these unholy affections, I should wish them banished. Nay, mere innocent pleasure is not a sufficient motive; the glory of God must be the end and aim of every attainment, or else it is a waste of time, and an abuse of talent. Pencils, paint, India-ink, and India-rubber, may be devoted to the honor of Him who bestows the power of combining their respective properties, so as to produce the similitudes of his works. I am no less anxious about the cultivation of musical talents; there is, however, more danger of music being abused than drawing: the inundation of frivolity, and the sometimes unsuspected associations of a carnal and worldly nature, which mingle with musical compositions of a modern and fashionable cast, often distress and hurt me. The fascinations of the ballroom, the corruptions of the theater and opera-house, too often creep into the quiet piano-forte corner of young people. Even instrumental music, with its appendages of waltzes, dances, and love-sick airs, has often a tendency to familiarize the young mind with subjects injurious to its welfare. The sober dignity of genuine instrumental music, is nearly lost in the substitution of modern trick and blandishment: but if instrumental music be thus abused, how much more so vocal: here the art and science of music opens its richest stores of opportunity for glorifying God and edifying man; here all the charms, and all the contrivances of this sublime faculty, present innumerable means of spiritualizing the heart, gratifying the ear, exalting the understanding, and improving the affections; but here, alas, the world, the flesh, and the devil have grasped the powers of the musical art in too many instances, and sacrificed them all to Dagon and Baal, to vice and folly, to levity and wantonness, to fascination and delusion. Love-songs, drinking-songs, vice-provoking songs, and many other sorts of songs, resound from house to house in public and private, and prove to demonstration the idols which men and even women serve, and consequently "whose they are." What a profanation of a holy art; what a degradation of a noble science. I am persuaded that music is designed to prepare for heaven, to educate for the choral enjoyment of paradise, to form the mind to virtue and devotion, and to charm away evil and sanctify the heart to God. A Christian musician is one who has a harp in his affections, which he daily tunes to the notes of the angelic host, and with which he makes melody in his heart to the Lord. Does he strike the chord with his hands? it is to "bid lute and harp to awake to the glory of God." The hand, the tongue, and the ear form a kind of triple chord not to be broken. Bring music, my beloved Fanny, to this test, and your vocal hours will not be spent in vain. The instructions of your childhood will supply you through life with a fountain of pleasures, drawn from the true source of legitimate recreation. Sing the songs of Zion, and amidst the vibrations of the air may true prayer and praise ascend to heaven, and enter into the ears of the Lord God of your salvation; and then will the harmonious combination be complete. Pray for grace to guide you in all your duties, that you may comfort, assist, and strengthen your invaluable mother in all her cares and labors, by your dutiful, diligent, and affectionate regard to her precepts, example, and wishes. May your brothers in particular learn from you, and you from Christ, what Christian meekness, activity, and sobriety mean. Watch over them with a sister's heart and a sister's prayers, and they will be heard and answered. Go to school again and again. Whither? To what school, papa? To the school of Christ, where the great Instructor waits to teach and bless you. Go thither, my child, and carry your sins, and your cares, and your weaknesses, and your errors, and your affections, and your hopes, and your fears, and your resolutions, and your friends, and your brothers, and your sisters, and your mother, and

Your own true loving father,

LEGH RICHMOND

*To his eldest Son.*

MY DEAR LITTLE BOY—You cannot think how glad I was to see your letter; so glad that it made me weep: if you knew how dearly I love you, I am sure you would dearly love me; and if you knew how dearly God loves you, you would love him also. Never forget God, for he is always thinking about you; do you not see how good he is to you, in giving you a papa and mamma, and sisters, and friends, and a house to live in, and food, and so many other good things?

I preached a sermon last Sunday, to some hundreds of little children, and you can hardly think how well they behaved, and how silently and closely they attended to what they heard. Many of them, when they returned home, wrote down what they heard from me at church: when will you do so, my dear Nugent? I hope you get your lesson well for Mr. D——; how kind he is to teach you. I hope you pray for me every day; I often pray for you, and God will hear both you and me, if we pray with our whole hearts. When you have read this letter, you must go and kiss M. and F. and H., and tell them I bid you do so for me, because I am far away, and cannot give them myself a proof of my affection for them.

My Nugent, you are the eldest; if you are a good child, they may follow your example, and if you are a bad boy, it will teach them to be sinful; and that will make God very angry, and me very unhappy. You are now every day growing older, and you ought to grow wiser and better, and then you will be a comfort to us all, and I shall rejoice and praise. I wish you tomorrow morning to read the tenth chapter of St. Mark, and you will see how Jesus Christ loved little children, and how he took them up in his arms and blessed them. I hope he will bless you, and then you will go to heaven when you die; but without a blessing from Christ you never can go there. I trust I shall see you again soon. You must pray to God to bring me back in health and safety. I have written to you as long a letter as perhaps you will like to read: one thing only I will add, that

I am your true loving papa,

L. R.

We here insert a specimen of the happy manner in which Mr. Richmond combined instruction and amusement—religious truth and scientific knowledge. It is a meditation on the wonders of a kaleidoscope, which he presented to his daughter Fanny, with a view to engage her attention to this simple and elegant instrument.

My dear Fanny—See what this new discovery, which has afforded us so much amusement, may do to improve our heads and hearts.

I took up my kaleidoscope, and as I viewed with delight the extraordinary succession of beautiful images which it presented to my sight, I was struck,

1. With the singular phenomenon of perfect order being invariably and constantly produced out of perfect disorder; so that, as by magical influence, confusion and irregularity seemed to become the prolific parents of symmetry and beauty.

2. It occurred to me, that the universality of its adoption would imperceptibly lead to the cultivation of the principles of taste, elegance, and beauty, through the whole of the present and following generations; and that from the philosopher and artist down to the poorest child in the community.

3. I admired the effects produced by new and varied combinations of colors as well as forms. The analysis of this kind of arrangement is here attended with unprecedented facility and advantage. The artist, the philosopher, the admirer both of the works of nature and of art, may find a source of amusement almost peculiar to the use of this instrument.

4. I saw a vast accession to the sources of invention in its application to the elegant arts and manufactures, and the consequent growth of a more polished and highly cultivated state of habits, manners, and refinement in both.

5. I mused with delight on the powers and effects of geometrical arrangement and combination, so easily exhibited to the eye, and so characteristic of the optical principle on which the instrument is constructed.

6. I was struck with the idea of infinite variety, more strikingly demonstrated to the eye than by any former experiment. Here the

sublime mingles with the beautiful.

7. I perceived a kind of visible music. The combination of form and color produced harmony, their succession melody; thus, what an organ or piano-forte is to the ear, the kaleidoscope is to the eye. I was delighted with this analogy between the senses, as exercised in this interesting experiment.

8. I thought that God was very good to afford and permit so innocent and gratifying a source of recreation to all ranks of my fellow-countrymen, arising partly from the exhibition of so much loveliness to that sense of sight which he has formed, and partly from the exercise of the mental faculties of reason and taste in meditating upon the beautiful vision.

I laid my kaleidoscope down, and thought of the adorable attributes of Him from whom all blessings, earthly and heavenly, flow.

I took up my kaleidoscope again, and was led, in the contemplation of its use and beauties, to think,

1. Here I seem to see, on the one hand, the ruin and disorder of human nature, and on the other, the marvellous influence of grace in producing, out of these materials, order, beauty, and restoration.

2. My instrument I compared to a telescope-glass, which faith and hope put into my hand. I saw, through one end of the tube, the world and our life in it, a scene of confusion and tribulation, strange revolutions and mysterious complexities. Through the other, I beheld promised delights, heavenly realities, beauty for ashes, and the wilderness blooming like a rose. I took the hint, and saw reasons for resignation, contentment, and patient waiting for the glory that shall be revealed.

3. I observed, as I gently turned my instrument round, how quickly the pleasure of sense vanished. The phantom which delighted me but a moment before, was gone, for ever gone, irrecoverably lost. Let me not then, said I, set my heart on that which so quickly taketh wing and fleeth away. Such is the world and its delights.

4. But again, as I looked, new beauties constantly succeeded those which had passed away. Now, I thought, how does the Lord

multiply his mercies in constant variety and succession. In the succession of beautiful configurations in my glass, is an emblem of the endless goodness of my God, whose tender mercies are over all his works.

5. In this chaos of confusion, thus made to produce beauty and order, I seem to see a representation of the primitive work of the great Creator, who, when the earth was without form and void, sent forth his Spirit, and therewith created an universe in all its original perfection.

6. When I look at my little fragments of glass and stones, and observe how, from such apparently despicable materials, such beauty and symmetry arise, I learn not to despise the day of small things, and to count nothing unworthy of my notice. I learn how God has chosen the foolish things of this world to confound the wise; and base things of this world, and things which are despised, hath God chosen, yea, things which are not, to bring to naught things that are: that no flesh should glory in his presence.

I concluded by reflecting, how the works of creation, the principles of natural philosophy, the discoveries of science, and the ingenuities of art, illustrate and demonstrate the attributes of the God of redemption. My kaleidoscope shows me, in the harmony of its colors, the union of his excellencies; in the symmetry of its forms, his wisdom; in the invariable efficacy of its principles, his faithfulness; in the endless diversity of its figures, his infinity; in the simplicity of its essential character, his unity; in its faculty of producing novelty, his power; in its ability to delight, his goodness; and in its affording me this opportunity of so seeing him in it, his love.

I laid down my kaleidoscope, that I might praise and pray to the Author of my mercies.

## Chapter 2

LETTERS TO HIS SON WILBERFORCE—TO HIS CHILDREN,
EMBRACING A MEMORIAL OF HIS MOTHER—BIRTHDAY
LETTERS TO HIS CHILDREN—TO HIS THIRD DAUGHTER,
DURING AN ATTACK OF ILLNESS—NOTES TO THE SAME—
LETTER TO HIS ELDEST DAUGHTER—NOTES TO HIS
CHILDREN—LETTERS TO WILBERFORCE ON THE SUBJECT
OF THE MINISTRY—TO HIS DAUGHTER FANNY

he two following letters are to the second son of Mr. Richmond, then in his twelfth year.

MY DEAR WILBERFORCE—Shall I have no cause for heartache at my return, when I inquire how my child has behaved; how he has attended to his learning; how he has adhered to truth in his words? Shall I be comforted with the glad tidings that your heart, and your conscience, and your ways, all seem to partake of a happy influence? That you show your love to mamma by keeping her commandments? That you pray to God to forgive your sins, and hourly offenses? Do the four walls of your little chamber bear witness to your prayers and supplications for yourself and me? Do the sun's rays, as they early penetrate your window in the morning, find you early and active to rise, to read, to labor, and to grow in grace?

I saw Lichfield cathedral, and attended divine service there. It is a much smaller one than York, but has great beauty; the organ-notes rolled sublimely through the vaults, arches, pillars, and roof; and the exquisitely painted windows assimilated with such sounds, and rendered the effect very fine. It has three beautiful spires.

One evening I travelled with a friend for three hours, amidst the most beautiful and never-ceasing distant lightning; the whole western hemisphere was in a constant blaze; the flashes alternated from one point of the horizon to another, distant about forty-five degrees from it: sometimes the flashes were silvery, sometimes yellow, sometimes orange; sometimes forked, sometimes sheet-like; sometimes so vivid, you seemed to have a peep into more distant regions of space; sometimes more faint; now and then you heard slight rumblings, then all was silent. At one point the flashes gleamed upon a distant view of a castle, which seemed all on fire, and was only rendered visible by the effect of the lightning. A dark forest lay behind, and formed a fine contrast. Sometimes the forked flashes hurried one another in a kind of playful progress; at others, they dashed together as if in terrible combat: all this passed between seven and ten o'clock, on the evening of June 28. But what are these lightnings, compared with those which made Moses quake and tremble at Mount Sinai? or what were even the latter, when contrasted with those of God's wrath against sinners? Thunder and lightning is a fine emblem of divine justice and threatenings. You have need to "flee from the wrath to come."[1] "Repent, for the kingdom of heaven is at hand."[2] "The wicked, and all the people that forget God, shall be turned into hell."[3] Do you forget him? if so, what shall be your portion? If you say you do not forget him, how do you prove it?

——video meliora proboque—
Deteriora sequor,[4]

is the character of too many nominal Christians; I would not have it to be yours. An enlightened but unconverted mind has eyes and tongue to approve what is right; but the feet follow the paths of evil. A converted heart alone walks in the steps of Him who is "the way, the truth, and the life." Say,

To me, O Lord, be thou "the way,"
To me, be thou "the truth";
To me, my Saviour, be "the life,"

---

1 Luke 3:7.
2 Matthew 3:2.
3 Psalm 9:17.
4 I see the right and approve it, yet pursue the wrong. (*Original footnote*)

Thou Guardian of my youth.

So shall that "way" be my delight,
That "truth" shall make me free;
That "life" shall raise me from the dead,
And then I'll live to thee.

I sincerely hope you are beginning to be truly sensible of the danger of sin, and the necessity of seeking the Lord very early. Your life is an uncertainty, at best; occasional indispositions should remind you that you may never arrive at man's estate. If you are to die a boy, we must look for a boy's religion, a boy's knowledge, a boy's faith, a boy's Saviour, a boy's salvation; or else, a boy's ignorance, a boy's obstinacy, a boy's unbelief, a boy's idolatry, a boy's destruction. Remember all this, and beware of sin; dread the sinfulness of an unchanged heart; pray for a new one; pray for grace and pardon, and a soul conformed to the image of Christ Jesus; pray for wisdom, for the destruction of pride, vain conceit, and self-sufficiency. "Be not slothful in business; but fervent in spirit, serving the Lord."[1]

Friends here inquire after you; but it is in the full hope that you go on well, creditably, obediently, industriously, humbly, and Christianly. Love to all, from

Your affectionate father,

L. R.

We here introduce a birthday hymn, composed for his son Wilberforce.

My years roll on in silent course,
Impelled by a resistless force:
Awake, my soul, awake and sing,
How good thy God, how great thy King.

My years roll on: then let me know
The great design for which they flow;
And as the ship floats o'er the wave,
Thy vessel, Lord, in mercy save.

---

1 Romans 12:11.

My years roll on: the tide of time
Bears me through many a changing clime:
I've summers, winters—heat and cold—
Winds, calms, and tempests, ten times told.

My years roll on: but here's my hope,
And this my everlasting prop:
Though seasons change, and I change too,
My God's the same—for ever true.

My years roll on; and as they roll,
Oh, may they waft my ransomed soul
Safe through life's ocean, to yon shore,
Where sins and sorrows grieve no more.

My years roll on; and with them flows
That mercy which no limit knows:
'Tis Mercy's current makes me glide,
In hope of safety, down the tide.

My years roll on: my soul be still—
Guided by love, thy course fulfil:
And, my life's anxious voyage past,
My refuge be with Christ at last!

L. R.

MY DEAR BOY—Were I to attempt to describe the beauties of the highlands of Scotland to you, I should be much at a loss. Whether my subject were the grand mountains, with snow still on their tops; or the magnificent waterfalls, amidst rocks, and glens, and woods; or the noble rivers and romantic brooks, winding through fruitful plains or hills; or the fine lakes expanding their bosoms to the clouds, which they reflect from their surfaces; whether I were to write from the splendid mansion and grounds of a highland chief, or the lowly, smoke-dried cottage of a highland peasant; whether the ruined castle or abbey, or the neat modern parish church, were the subject of my description, I could say much, yet not enough. Here I am, amidst the unexampled and wild beauties of the Trosacks, on the banks of Loch Katrine. *There* is the glen, down which Fitz-James hurried from the mountains, when he lost his way: *there* is the island of the Lady of the Lake, from whence she put forth her little skiff, at the sound of the echoing horn. *There* is the great mountain of Benvenu, springing up from the lake to the clouds: there is his brother Benan, with Benean, and Benhaum, and Benledi, and Benvoirlicn, and Beneen, and many more lofty beins, (mountains) surrounding this most lovely lake. Here is the Goblin's Hole; and *there* the spot where the last of the couriers of Roderic Dhu was slain. In all the scene sublimity reigns; and, above all, God reigns in it also.

*To his daughter Fanny.*

MY DEAR FANNY—I was unspeakably gratified at Newcastle, in seeing two little girls, one of ten, the other of twelve, the spiritual fruits of my "Young Cottager"; the latter of the two I had not seen before. I never before, except in the case of "Little Jane" herself, saw so clear and so early an instance of decided grace, and of a truly enlightened mind: you would have thought, her conversation equal to eighteen at least. I apprehend that I have become acquainted with above thirty cases of decided usefulness in youth, from that Tract, since I came into the north. Oh, what a mercy. In this, "goodness indeed follows me."

My visit to Scotland has been marked by more affection and usefulness than any one I ever made: numerous public and private occurrences overwhelm me with gratitude. The Scottish scenery is of the very first class. Whatever is beautiful, whatever is grand, whatever is wild and romantic—all are to be found in almost unlimited variety of display. Noble rivers, lakes, and waterfalls, picturesque hills and mountains, lovely land and sea views, fine towns and buildings—all speaking the goodness, power, and wisdom of God. The marks of affection, regard, and esteem, with which I was received, far exceed what I have ever witnessed; and I have reason to believe much actual good was done to many individuals, while I was there.

After the death of Mr. Richmond's mother, in 1819, he prepared a memorial of her virtues, in a series of letters addressed to his children, from two of which we give the following selections. Reference is here made to his eldest son Nugent, who unhappily falling into the company of depraved and vicious young men, was led into evil habits, and induced to make choice of a seafaring life, to which his father most reluctantly consented. Accordingly, at the age of sixteen, he embarked in a merchant vessel, destined to Ceylon, and arrived at Colombo in January, 1815.

My beloved Children—The affecting summons which I so lately and unexpectedly received, to pay the last act of duty and love to the remains of my invaluable and revered parent, has impressed my mind with a strong desire to leave some memorial of her character, for your sakes and for your instruction.

I am just returned from the grave of one whom a thousand tender recollections endeared to every faculty of my soul: and I wish to preserve something of that solemnity of feeling, and gratitude of heart, which such a scene was calculated to inspire. How can I better do this, than by endeavoring to convey those emotions to *your* bosoms, through the medium of an epistolary communication, devoted to an affectionate retrospect of the character and disposition of the deceased? I feel myself, as it were, a debtor to two generations, between whom I now stand, as the willing, though feeble and unworthy agent, by whom benefits and consolations, derived from the one, may be transferred for the lasting advantage of the other. The solid character of her religious principles, the superiority of her mental attainments, and the singularly amiable deportment by which she was distinguished, constitute powerful claims to *your* regard. If any additional plea were needed, I would derive it from the deep and affectionate interest which she took in whatever concerned your welfare, both spiritual and temporal; from the prayers which she daily offered up to the throne of mercy for *your* happiness, and from the unceasing watchfulness and anxiety which she manifested for *your* progress in every good word and work.

Although she was far separated from you, by the distance of her residence from our own, and the opportunities of personal intercourse were thereby greatly restricted, yet her most tender and sacred affections were ever near to me and mine. We occupied her daily thoughts and her nightly meditations; and now that she is gone to rest, and her heart can no longer beat with mortal anxieties, it is highly becoming that we who loved her, and whom she so ardently loved, should give a consistency to our affection for such a parent, by a grateful inquiry into those qualities of head and heart with which God so eminently blessed her.

There is a solitary tree, underneath which, by her own desire, she lies buried, in Lancaster churchyard. I feel a wish, if I may be allowed for a moment to employ the imagery, to pluck a branch from this tree that waves over her tomb; to transplant it into my own domestic garden, and there behold it flourish, and bring forth "fruit-unto holiness." I would gladly encourage a hope that this wish may be realized in you, my children, and that such intercourse with the dead may indeed prove a blessing to the living.

But this can be expected only in dependence on the free and undeserved mercy of that God and Saviour in whom your venerable grandmother trusted, and "whom to know is life eternal." Whatever, therefore, of domestic narrative; whatever of earnest exhortation to yourselves; or whatever of remark upon the interesting qualities of the subject of this memoir, may intermingle with my present address, keep invariably in mind, that my great object, as it concerns her, and you, and myself, is to give glory to God alone; and in the deepest humiliation of heart, to look up to him as the sole fountain of excellence.

In addressing you on such a subject, my children, it is natural that I should reflect on the varieties of age and circumstance in which you are placed. Even in point of your *number*, I can hardly pronounce it without some degree of fear and trembling. *Ten* immortal souls: souls allied to my own, by ties inexpressibly tender, and inviolably dear: souls committed to my charge, not only as a minister, but also as a parent. "Who is sufficient for these things?"[1] has been the secret cry of many a minister and many a parent. In each of these relations, I wish to apply that divine promise to my heart, "our sufficiency is of God." I have long cherished a hope, founded on another gracious intimation of his will to those who love and fear him, "The promise is unto you, and to your children, and to all that are afar off, even as many as the Lord our God shall call."[2] Supported by these consolations, it has been my aim to bring you up in the nurture and admonition of the Lord, and to train up my children in the right way; trusting, that if they live to be old, they will not depart from it. Yet sometimes the anxious fear, connected with a survey of the world in which you are placed—its vanities and its vices, its delusions and its dangers—will force itself on my thoughts. I have lived to see, in other families, some of their buds of promise blighted, through the baneful and infectious influence of corrupt associations. I have seen what havoc the pomps and vanities of this wicked world, the sinful lusts of the flesh, and the wiles of the devil, have made in many a household. I have witnessed the sorrows, and mingled mine with the tears of my friends, when they have spoken of the wanderings and misconduct of some of their children: and then, I have occasionally trembled for my own little flock. But I feel it, at the same time, to be both my privilege and my duty to use this very solicitude for a higher and nobler purpose than despondency and unbelief would suggest. These anxious affections are planted in the parental heart, and manifestly ordained of God, as incentives to caution and stimulants to prayer. As such, I would employ them for your sakes; I would thereby the more assiduously teach you to "abhor that which is evil, and cleave to that which is good":[3] and above all, I would with the more earnestness and dependence on the covenant grace of God, present your mortal and immortal interests, in supplication to him who hath said, "The

---

1  2 Corinthians 2:16.
2  Acts 2:39.
3  Romans 12:9.

promise is unto you, and to your children, and to all that are afar off, as many as the Lord shall call."

And surely, I may be allowed to urge an excuse for dwelling upon this text, even in a way of literal application. For you, my first-born child, are indeed "afar off"; and these pages may much more easily reach you, amongst your uncertain journeyings on the shores or the waves of India, than they can ever convey an adequate idea of the exercises of varied affection, which your eventful history has occasioned us.

Next to your immediate parents, no one felt so deeply on your account as my deceased mother. Her prayers and good wishes were mingled with our own, when we first committed you to the vicissitudes of the ocean, and the mariner's lot; and the above named promise was her support, as well as ours.

As I stood on the shores of the Isle of Wight, in the summer of 1814, and watched the departure of the ship which contained my child, with a father's eye and a father's heart, I mused over the past, the present, and the future, until the shadows of the night interrupted my view. One moment suggested, "my poor child will soon be *afar off*"; the next, as it were, replied, but "the promise is unto you, and to your children, and to as many as are *afar off*." The thought consoled me as I returned homeward, and I prayed for my little ones, that God would "speak peace to you which were afar off, and to them that were nigh."[1]

And then, again, my son, when during the following year we received the dismal tidings of the wreck of your ship, and the destruction of nearly all her crew, on the coast of Africa, as she returned on her voyage from Ceylon, when among the six persons whom alone, out of three hundred and sixty, Providence saved from death, we found not your name, we seemed, in this valley of the shadow of death, more than ever to need the rod and the staff of the great Shepherd to comfort us. At that trying period the same promise came to our aid, and we felt its consoling influence; while,

1 Ephesians 2:17.

like Aaron, when his sons were dead, we held our peace. And when afterwards it pleased God, in the mystery of his mercies, to discover to us our mistake, and to prove to us that you had no part in the horrors of this watery grave, it did indeed seem once more fulfilled, "This my son was dead, and is alive again; he was lost, and is found."[1]

During these transitions of feeling, I cannot express how much the truly scriptural communication of sentiments and counsel, which we received from my now deceased parent, contributed to the encouragement of faith, and patience, and gratitude. From that period till her death, the welfare of my child "afar off" continued to lay very near to her heart. "What news from India?" was her frequent inquiry, and always accompanied by the interesting tear of maternal solicitude. To you, therefore, as the eldest of my dear filial flock, I may, with due earnestness, first commend this "tribute of affectionate veneration for the memory of my deceased mother."

She was a faithful mother to us all; and I wish her memory to be enshrined in the grateful recollection of your heart. If these lines are ever permitted to meet your perusal, my son, cherish them, for her sake and mine.

From India, I turn to my nine children at home, and greet you with a father's blessing, as I present you with these domestic meditations, which I write for the sake of those of you who have enjoyed the opportunity of occasional intercourse with the subject of the memoir, as well as of those whom circumstances never permitted to know her. I anticipate the time when even my last born, the babe that cannot yet lisp the honored name of "grandmother," shall not be ignorant of her worth, but shall love to listen to the record of those gracious affections with which God was pleased to adorn her: and perhaps, on some future day, when visiting the grave where she is laid, may say, "Here lies one, whom from my cradle I was taught to love and honor."

But, whilst I am enumerating "the olive-branches which

1 Luke 15:24.

surround my table," and "the children whom God hath given me," I suddenly feel as if I had erred in my calculations. Is there no link of connection between the visible and invisible worlds; no right of appropriation by which an earthly parent may say, "I have a child in heaven?" Yes, a sweet little cherub in the mansions above seems to my imagination to be the very link which faith and love would employ to animate all the energies of my best affections, when I look at my still living children, and contemplate their immortal condition.

One of you, my *eleven* children, is in glory—a lamb, safely and eternally folded in the arms of his Redeemer. He is the first of my household that has gone to his rest. May he prove a pledge for many to follow him there, in God's own time. In the meantime, cherish it in your frequent remembrance, as an argument for heavenly-mindedness, that one of you is already in heaven. I may not, indeed, now address myself to *him;* but I may speak of him to you; I may remind you of his epitaph, and of the paradise to which he belongs. I may also thus preserve the sense of kindred alliance between the dead and the living of my family, and ardently pray for the perfect and eternal reunion of them all, through grace, in "the house not made with hands, eternal in the heavens."[1] Such, likewise, were the supplications of her who, through faith and patience, is gone to inherit the promises, and to join our own little infant in singing hallelujahs "to him that sitteth upon the throne, and unto the Lamb."[2]

In the cherished anticipation of such results, from the free and undeserved mercies of redemption, I will conclude the present letter, by subscribing myself

Your affectionate father,

LEGH RICHMOND

\*    \*    \*    \*

The conduct of your grandmother during the single state, as

---

1  2 Corinthians 5:1.
2  Revelation 5:13.

a daughter, had been useful, affectionate, dutiful, and domestic. Such daughters, and such alone, are calculated to exhibit those still brighter characteristics which attach to the subsequent relations of the wife and the mother. Let my children ever remember, that *in the ordinary course of the progress of a Christian and domestic character, the seed of hope is planted in childhood, and the bud manifests its first beauty and fragrance in their earlier youth, and thence issues that more expanded foliage, which constitutes the ornamental features of their more advanced condition.* There is a wise and beautiful order in the mode and manner of the dispensations of God's grace.

There is a progressive attainment of knowledge, and a growth of principle in the hearts of such as he is training up in the way they should go, which successively develop as the infant advances to childhood, the child to youth, and the youth to man. There is a preparation of heart which accompanies this progressive formation of character. The affections and principles of action which, under the divine blessing, have been fostered in the bosom of the child, to the furtherance of the parent's happiness, and the general welfare of the domestic circle, are precisely those which will hereafter constitute the solidity and the loveliness of the nuptial character. The difficulties and the trials of early life may have been fewer—mercifully, perhaps, ordained to be so—but the heart that has been disciplined in the school of filial obedience and affection, is thus prepared for future usefulness, and for the trial of faith, love, and patience, in a subsequently acquired relation.

More particularly to speak of the female character: subject to those exceptions which the unlimited grace of the Almighty is sometimes pleased to make in the dispositions of individuals at a more advanced period of life—exceptions which in no respect form a rule for general conclusions: those who, in unaffected sobriety of manners and simple spirituality of heart, have aimed at fulfilling the domestic duties of the *daughter*, will ever constitute that truly honorable class of women whom Providence appoints to sustain the more arduous characters of the *Christian wife* and the *Christian mother*. In vain shall we look for characters of this description among the daughters of folly and fashion. Their hearts are estranged from the very principle of the domestic disposition. Accustomed to the repeated indulgence of luxurious inclinations, their volatile desires are ever upon the wing, in search of something new and gay, that may satisfy a craving and disordered appetite for novelties. They are "lovers of pleasure more than lovers of God." But, says the same apostle, "she that liveth in pleasure is dead while she liveth."[1] Beware, my dear daughters, of such examples; dread their contagion, and, therefore, shun their society. . . . Let it be the comfort of my advancing years, to see that your center of attachment, as well as duty, is *at home*. Numberless and invaluable are the ideas which connect with that one word, *home*. May you and I so cherish them by sacred principle on earth, that we may be found meet for a better home hereafter, even for "the inheritance of the saints in light."[2]

### *To his second Daughter.*

MY DEAR FANNY—I am just returned, after executing the difficult and affecting task of preaching a funeral sermon for my most excellent and revered mother, at her parish church. I took my subject from Psalm 115:1, as best suited to her humble, meek, and believing frame of mind. It was indeed a trying effort; but God carried me through surprisingly. I introduced some very interesting papers, which I have found amongst her memoranda, in her own handwriting. Her last message to me was, "Tell my son, I am going direct to happiness."

Never was there a more delightful and heavenly countenance than hers, as she lay in her coffin; it combined every sentiment which the most devout mind could desire: love, joy, peace, gentleness, goodness, faith, meekness, charity, all shone serenely bright. I followed her to her grave, in Lancaster church-yard, where she lies under a sycamore-tree, amid the magnificent landscape of sea,

---

1  1 Timothy 5:6.
2  Colossians 1:12.

mountains, rivers, castle, and church around. You remember its high beauties. But you very imperfectly know the high qualities of head and heart which your grandmamma possessed; I never met with her equal at the same age. I occupy her little room, adjoining her bedroom, by day; and it is a great consolation to me to sit in her arm-chair and think of her, and read her papers on various subjects. There you and I took leave of her, in November last; but alas, her place knoweth her no more. I look out of the window, at the grand range of snow-capt mountains, which are now beautiful in the extreme. I had no conception of the winter beauties of these hills: Lansdale Piles, Rydal Head, Hill Bell, Helvellyn, etc., etc., all finely illuminated with snow-sunshine, in diversified shades. And then I think of my dear mother, and how she enjoyed their characteristic grandeur.

Letters pour in daily, from all parts of England, condoling with us in our great loss. My mother was loved and honored most extensively. Dear woman, for forty-seven years I have proved thy affection, and can trace, from earliest infancy, the tokens of thy worth. May I follow thee in humility, faith, and love; and cherish thy memory with gratitude and honor.

The two next letters are to one of his younger children, written on her birthday in successive years.

To MY K——, Let not my loved little K—— suppose that her father forgets her. Yaxham may seem a long distance from Turvey; Glasgow is much greater; but in neither place can my heart forget my child. I remember you a little babe, in arms. I loved you then. I remember you lying in your little cot, and I swung you there, and loved you the while.

I recollect your first attempts to walk, and your many consequent little downfalls. I raised you up from your stumblings and your tumblings; I dried your tears, and loved you still more. I have not forgotten your endeavors to talk, nor your droll little prattlings;

nor your first calling me papa, and dearly I loved you for it: and although these things have long since passed away, and time has added to your years, my love for my K—— is not diminished. I often see you in imagination, and draw fanciful pictures of your occupations in your new dwelling. But what is my love compared with that of your heavenly Father? What is the strongest earthly affection, when contrasted with that which said, "Suffer little children to come unto me, and forbid them not; for of such is the kingdom of heaven?"[1] Has my child's heart an earnestness, a real unfeigned earnestness, to share in the love of such a Father, and to come when so mercifully called to such a Saviour? By nature, "foolishness is bound up in the heart of a child";[2] nevertheless, by grace a young child's heart may become the temple of the Holy Ghost, and the residence of God himself. Think of little Jane, the young cottager. May you resemble her in whatever she resembled Christ. She was a dear little girl, and I wish there were thousands more like her. Many have been made sensible of their sinful state while reading that story, and, through the blessing of God, have been brought to love the same Redeemer, and lived and died rejoicing in their Saviour. I hope, my child, you pray not only with your lips, but with your heart. While you are actively and dutifully employed in acquiring useful knowledge, "be fervent in spirit, serving the Lord."[3] In a little time you will be in your teens, and the very sound of that word should awaken you, not to the usual folly and vanity of this period of life, but to the responsibility of growing years and increasing privileges; to the cultivation of holy learning and Christian habits; to the love of Jesus and communion with his Spirit. It is *my* prayer, let it be *yours*. And now farewell, my dear K——. May you realize every fond hope, temporal, spiritual, and eternal, of

Your affectionate father,

L. R.

---

1 Matthew 19:14.

2 Proverbs 22:15.

3 Romans 12:11.

To my K——, on her birthday—Accept a birthday blessing from your affectionate father, my dearest K——: a father who loves you with all his heart and soul. This day thirteen years brought you into a world of sins, sorrows, mercies, hopes, and fears: surely, it is a day much to be remembered; not so much by feastings and twelfth-cakes, as by prayers and supplications to the God and Father of our Lord Jesus Christ, that he would grant you grace to put away the follies of childhood, and to enter upon what is commonly called your "teens" with a clean heart and a right spirit. May my dear child be a vessel of mercy, filled with all the blessings of the Spirit of God, and fitted for a happy eternity. May the love of Jesus warm your heart with every affection which can adorn the Christian name and character. May your early attainments at this period of diligent childhood prepare you to be the comfort and prop of your parents in their advancing years, if life be spared to them. Be conscientious in all you do. Idleness and inattention to instruction always prove that something is very wrong in the principle. Diligence in the improvement of your mind is a tribute of obedience both to God and your parents. I rejoice to hear from your kind governess that you improve in this respect. I trust, my dear child, we shall never receive any intimation of your failure in so important a matter. If you love those at home—and I am persuaded you do love them tenderly—ever strive to make them happy and easy on your account. I need not tell you, that every one round our fireside unites with me in the congratulations of this day. There is but one heart amongst us. M—— and H—— mention your birthday in their letters. Our Christian circle is reduced when three daughters are absent, but love, memory, and imagination often bring them all together, and half fill the vacant chairs which they used to occupy. Your brother Nugent has been mercifully preserved from an awful shipwreck in India; the vessel was totally lost, but all the lives saved. And now, my K——, with a repetition, of every wish, prayer, and blessing, believe me

Your affectionate father,

L. R.

To C——, (when a very little girl)—Perhaps my dear little C—— thought she was too young to receive a letter; but you see I have not forgotten you. I wish very much to know how you are behaving since I saw you. What character will your pen and your needle give of you when I ask them; and what will your book say? Your playthings, perhaps, will whisper that you have been very fond of *them:* well, a little fond of them you may be, but you must not think *only* of them, my little-nursery queen. There are better things than playthings in the world: there are mammas, and mamma's commandments, and papas, and papa's wishes, and sisters, and sister's instructions; and there is the Bible, and the God of the Bible, and Jesus Christ and his salvation. My little girl must think of these things, and be an example to her young brothers, in order, obedience, and good manners, etc.

You are now at that age when Jesus "increased in wisdom and stature, and in favor with God and man."[1] Meditate on this. I am glad to think you are acquiring knowledge; but ever keep in mind, that all other knowledge is valuable, or not, just so far as it is united to spiritual knowledge. The word of God and its blessings form the highest study of man. May my children grow in such knowledge. Farewell, my child; try in every thing to please

Your dear,

PAPA

P. S.—I send a box of changeable ladies to amuse you, but I do not wish *you* to become one of the changeable ladies: yet my heart prays that you may prove a changed soul.

### ADDRESSED TO MISS RICHMOND:
ACCOMPANIED BY A LOCKET OF DERBYSHIRE FLUOR SPAR,
IN THE FORM OF A HEART

Here I offer my daughter a heart without sin,
That knows naught of corruption and sorrow within;
A heart which you see is so curiously wrought,

1 Luke 2:52.

That it ne'er can offend—not so much as in thought.

That its virtues are shining within and without,
Is a truth which admits of no rational doubt;
Its character, Mary, is pure and sincere,
And its inmost ideas transparent and clear.

'Tis a heart that will bear the minutest inspection,
And never prove guilty of any deception:
What it was, that it is—what it is, it will be—
Unconscious of guile or to you or to me.

It may seem to be strange—nay, it is so, I own—
That this heart, though so pure, is as hard as a stone
It resists all impressions which tenderness makes,
But if force be employed, it immediately breaks.

And this heart, if once broken, can never be healed,
Nor the least of its wounds be a moment concealed;
And though stony its texture, and hard be its nature,
Like yourself, this poor heart is a delicate creature.

Then make use of the emblem you wear at your breast:
With "the hearts that are pure,"[1] do you seek to be blest;
Weep and mourn for a nature by sin so deranged,
And pray for a heart that's essentially changed.

May the "stone" in your heart be removed far away,
And the softened affections alone bear the sway:
They will lead you to Jesus with penitent sighs,
Till the sun of his righteousness sweetly arise.

May graces resplendent as those of the stone,
Both within and without, be for ever your own.
Let your heart be transparent, wherever you are,
And your conduct will shine far more clear than the spar.

But should you offend, and for sin be heart-broken,
Behold, on the cross there is Mercy's bright token.
The heart that is contrite God will not despise—
The heart that is broken is dear in his eyes.

Christ's love has no limit, then give him thy heart—

---

1 Matthew 5:8.

In the deed shall his Spirit free comfort impart:
So the heart of the Saviour, allied close to thine,
In a glorious unity ever will shine.

L. R.

*To his third daughter, Henrietta.*

DEAR HENRIETTA—And now comes your turn. Receive, read, mark, and inwardly digest. I do not know how much you are grown in stature, but I do hope you are growing in wisdom. Then, whether you are to be a woman tall, or a woman short, will signify very little. You will, if your wisdom be of the right kind, be of a tall mind and of tall attainments, and we will call you the little woman with the great soul. I have heard of a person's soul being so mean and small, that if you were to put it into a hollow mustard-seed and shake it well, it would rattle. Now, that is not the sort of soul I wish to discover in you. I want to see a soul in you which can embrace all useful and requisite knowledge—a soul which can extend its energies beyond ordinary limits—which can feel for all around you, and carry its benevolent activity throughout the universe—which can contemplate the globe, such a one as you study at B———, and find new problems upon it—as how to carry the Gospel into all latitudes and all longitudes—how to excite pity for the poor heathen in every zone and climate of the world—how to equalize all nations in the sympathy of Christian love, and thus make a spiritual equator—how to estimate the coldness of irreligion in the burning regions of the tropics, and how to carry the lively heat of evangelical charity into the districts of the poles. I would have you capable of grasping all these questions in your heart, with as much ease as your hands would clasp a doll, or as mine would clasp your own dear self to my bosom. But why do I wish that your soul may become thus capacious? Simply to this end—that you may thereby resemble Him who so loved the world, that he came into it to save sinners; yes, sinners, Henrietta, like unto you. Have you ever thought of this great truth as you ought? Is foolishness still bound up in the heart of my child? Is human existence only to be estimated by playthings, and holidays, and all the etceteras of a light-minded state? What, a young damsel almost fourteen years old, and no more progress in divine things. Study your Bible, and remember your privileges. Study your Bible, and dig deep for a foundation whereon to build your house. Study your Bible, and say what must become of all the thoughtless little girls in the world, if they do not repent and believe. Once more, study your Bible, and learn what you first owe to God, and then to your parents, and then to brothers and sisters, then to teachers, and then to school-fellows, and then to all mankind. Such a meditation will, with God's blessing, prove a merciful hour to your own soul, and for the sake of yours, to my soul also. I hope you will now pursue your education with earnestness. Now is the time to lay in a stock of useful knowledge. You cannot set too high a value on the advantages which you possess. Whether you eat or drink, or whatever you do, do all to the glory of God. Childhood and its vanities must speedily pass away, and you must have done with childish things. Learn to pray, and commit your whole soul and body to Christ. He is able to keep what you give into his hand, unto the great day when the secrets of all hearts shall be disclosed. You are now at the age at which little Jane did this. Are you like her? Are you as ready to meet your God as she was? Ask the question of your heart, and carry it to the throne of mercy, where all praying souls are made welcome. I hope you like the Bible-meeting at Northampton. I wish you early to cultivate a cordial interest in that great work—the greatest work of the age. In the day when Dame Eleanor's cross[1] was built, the Bible was unknown to the greatest part of the country. What a contrast now. The angel flies through heaven and earth, presenting it to all. The stone cross was once almost an idol; but the true cross proclaimed in the Bible, is the real Christian's ensign, prop, and delight. Farewell, dear love. I am

Your own dear father,

L. R.

---

1 This cross is erected about a mile from Northampton, and was once held in great veneration by Catholic devotees. *(Original footnote)*

*To the same on her birthday.*

DEAR HENRIETTA—The return of a birthday is a signal for gratitude. Fourteen years ago, as I sat in my little study at Brading, in the
Isle of Wight, about six in the morning, in came a woman bearing
in her arms a little baby, and wished me joy of the same—now, this
little baby was a little girl, and that little girl was my Henrietta, and
now is the fifteenth time that joy has been uttered from year to year
whenever that day was named. But what is joy? Is it only a holiday?
But what is joy? Is it only a game of play; is it merely a jumping, and
frisking, and running, and chattering, and doll-dressing, and merry-
making, and feast-keeping? Is this all the joy of a birthday? Away, far
away be all such feeble interpretations of the word. Then what is a
birthday joy? Is it not the joy of parents, when they see their children growing up in the fear of the Lord, and in the practice of holiness? Is it not the joy of the husbandman, when he sees his crop ripe
and plentiful, and offering the promise of harvest? Is it not the joy
of the gardener, when he perceives his young trees thrive, and blossom, and bear fruit? Is it not the joy of the mother-bird, when, after
all her watchings, and tremblings, and flutterings over the nest, she
sees her little ones begin to fly, and become capable of answering
the end of divine Providence in their creation? Is it not the joy of
the Christian instructor, when, after hours, and days, and months,
and years spent in warning, teaching, guiding, praying for, and
affectionately superintending the young pupil's best interests, that
pupil proves a living commentary on the precepts received, grows
in grace, and love, and humility, and activity, and obedience and
as a bud of promise cheers the hearts of surrounding friends with
prospects of usefulness through life in all its relative circumstances?
If such be the ingredients of birthday joy, when duly estimated,
may I be gratified in expressing my joy today, and can you also participate in joy thus appreciated? God bless you, my dear Henrietta,
on this day, and on every day. Time flies, opportunity flies, the
school-hour flies, childhood flies, all things are hastening to a grand
consummation; what a solemn thought. May my child conceive

and cherish it to the glory of God, and her own everlasting consolation. May Christ become to her a gracious Saviour, received, loved, and honored by her. Such is the prayer of her affectionate father,

L. R.

*To the same, on an occasion of indisposition.*

DEAR HENRIETTA—My anxious wish for your spiritual and temporal welfare induces me to express my thoughts to you in these little notes. I cannot tell you how much I desire that this season of sickness may be blessed of God to your present and everlasting good. This thought is continually before me, and I pray constantly to him that you may be inwardly strengthened by the power of his might. Examine yourself. Prove yourself. Bring your heart and all your thoughts before God, and make a solemn surrender of yourself to him. Employ with gratitude and patience the means which are prescribed for your recovery, but trust in him alone. Physicians can do nothing without his blessing on the medicines. I thank God for your last note, and shall be much pleased when you can and will write me another. Above all things, be much in prayer; in the watches of the night speak to God; in the events of the day, tell him how much you need and depend on him. In moments of weakness, ask him for strength; in seasons of pain, petition for contentment. He will of his riches abundantly supply your need. But you must deal faithfully with yourself, and humbly and perseveringly with him. Be not content with merely saying, Christ died for sinners. Try to get an evidence that you have a personal interest in him. This may be known by the state of your heart towards him. "We love him because he first loved us."[1] His love produces love, and our love to him proves that he has loved, and does love us. Are you ignorant? he is wisdom. Are you guilty? he is righteousness. Are you unholy? he is sanctification. Are you a captive? he is redemption. What is he not to the sinner? his strength is perfect in the believer's weakness. He was tempted in all points like as we are, and therefore knows

---

1  1 John 4:19.

how to succor them that are tempted. O, my child, if you can only cleave to him, and all that he is, and all he has promised to be, nothing can harm you. Meditate on these things, and may God make them quite and entirely your own. Now for a text for reflection. "In all our afflictions he was afflicted."[1]

Not a pang ever distressed our bodies, nor a trial our hearts, but Jesus has felt it; and he not only felt it in himself, but he feels it for and in us. What a consolation is here. This thought has supported thousands in their trouble. May it support you. Behold Christ in every thing, see him everywhere, acknowledge him in every trial; for he sympathizes in all the trials of them that are his. They have not one pain too many. Even sufferings will all work together for good to them that love him. I wish my loved Henrietta may see, feel, believe, and enjoy this encouraging thought, and make it her own. God love and bless you. So prays your affectionate father,

L. R.

*Note to the same.*

Dear Love—The heart of man is deceitful above all things, and desperately wicked; who can know it? So said the prophet of old, and so will every one say that knows the plague of his own heart. I want you to employ your whole time now in studying your heart, that you may increasingly feel the need of a Saviour. Who else can cleanse your heart, but he who died for its salvation? Do not be contented with a little religion, a little knowledge, a little hope. Press forward to the enjoyment of a great and gracious religion, much knowledge of Christ, and a glorious hope full of immortality. I am indeed most anxious that you may now in right earnest seek and find the Lord. "What must I do to be saved?" is a great question. How shall my deceitful heart be renewed? Whenever I die, whither shall I go? are all questions connected with it. Ask God with all your heart for a right answer.

Your affectionate father,

L. R.

---

1  Isaiah 63:9.

*To the same.*

DEAR CHILD—Your reminding me not to forget to write to you, leads me to hope that you read my little notes with a desire to profit by them. You do not know how anxious I am for your soul's good. What God designs for you in the present illness, I know not; but this I know, that you cannot be too earnest about your eternal state. You cannot mourn for sin too deeply. You cannot love Christ too affectionately. You cannot trust in his blood and righteousness too firmly. I want you to be a monument of mercy; a believing, loving, praying child. If God is pleased to restore you to health, may you adorn the doctrine which you have been taught; and if he should see good to remove you to another world, O may you sleep sweetly in Jesus. Be much in prayer: "Seek, and ye shall find." No favor is too great for God to grant. You are past the age of childish ignorance, and are now an accountable being.

My Henrietta, nothing will satisfy me short of your being a true child of God. What effect have recent events produced on your mind? What desires, what fears, what hopes, what views of sin and Christ? . . . May God make you a joy to your affectionate father,

L. R.

*To his daughter, Mary.*

MY DEAR MARY—We have had a very prosperous journey thus far. I am passing a few comfortable days with —— at this place. But, alas, this is a town in which, speaking of our own church, religion is little known. The inhabitants of all ranks think of nothing but money, folly, vanity, and dissipation: their evenings are spent in the unprofitable anxieties of the card-table, the ensnaring amusement of dancing, or the delusions and temptations of the playhouse; their mornings, in idle gossipings and waste of time. When I see these things, I feel satisfied that I have kept my dear children from such scenes, and such companions. Oh, how lamentable to contemplate a great town full of inhabitants, gentry, clergy, manufacturers, tradesmen, etc., living almost without God in the world;

error preached from the pulpits; no care for the souls of the people; no family prayer in the houses; no zeal for religion, unless, perhaps, it be now and then excited to abuse and ridicule all those who have any real love for God and their souls.

May my dear child be preserved from the defilements of a vain, dangerous, and destroying world. You know not, and I wish you never may know, its snares and corruptions. I was greatly affected in conversing with a family at ———, upon the marriage of their daughter, under the following circumstances: the father was an exemplary clergyman, the mother a most pious woman; they had brought up a family with strict attention to religious precepts and principles, and they were not without hope that their daughter had some piety.

A young man of property, but of no decided religious principle, became acquainted with her. Inattentive to the affectionate duties which she owed to her excellent parents, their feelings, and their advice, she suffered her mind to be led away into an attachment towards the young man. The parents were aware that his general habits and views would be uncongenial to their wishes for a daughter's spiritual welfare, and therefore objected. However, the daughter so far obtained her wishes, that a very reluctant consent was given to the marriage. The daughter, gradually led away into worldly company and amusements, has given up even the outward profession of religion, and now lives as the world lives. Yet she is not happy; and her parents are very unhappy. The daughter cannot help remembering the example, the exhortations, the prayers, the solicitudes, and the tears of her parents; but it is only with remorse, which she strives to drown in worldly company and carnal amusements. They wept over the case with me, which presents a proof of the sad consequences of young people giving way to hasty impressions, and yielding to connections not founded on a regard to the honor of God, gratitude to parents, and consistency with a religious profession. How needful is it that Christian parents, and Christian children, should be firm and conscientious in the important duty of encouraging connections for life *only* on Christian principles; what distress to families and what decays of hopeful character have resulted from a deficiency on this point. Let me warn my dear Mary against that unbecoming levity, with which many young people treat these subjects. Evil communications corrupt good manners, very especially in this matter. The love of Christ is the only safe ground of all motives, and all conduct. Where this is established, all is well. The lifeblood of Christianity then circulates through every vein of the soul, and health, strength, and purity of mind is the happy result. Fall down upon your knees before God, my Mary, praying that he would pour *that* love into your heart, till it become a constraining principle for the government of your thoughts and actions. This is the only remedy for all the diseases of the soul.

Beware of pride and self-conceit; of fretful tempers and discontent. Learn to quell impatience and obstinacy. Let your first, your very first delight be in serving God by serving your parents. Reckon not on youth, or long life. Devote yourself to active usefulness in the family, and in the parish. Show forth the principles in which you have been educated, by a practical exhibition of them in your conduct. But who is sufficient unto these things? *Christ.* Without him you can do nothing; no, not so much as think a good thought. But you can do all things through Christ strengthening you. He is the sufficiency of all his people. By faith in him you obtain power to perform duty. By grace are ye saved, and that not of yourselves; not of works, lest any one should boast. Could works save us, we might boast, and heaven would be full of boasters. But no, no, no; the song of the saints is, "Not unto us, not unto us, but unto thy name be all the glory."[1]

Your affectionate father,

LEGH RICHMOND

*Note to his third Son.*

DEAR H——, Your text today shall be, "the blood of Jesus Christ cleanseth from all sin."[2] No sin is too great to be pardoned;

1 Psalm 115:1.
2 1 John 1:7.

but then the soul must seek, believe, and experience this mercy. There is infinite value in the blood of Christ, but the believer alone enjoys the privilege. "Believe on the Lord Jesus Christ, and thou shalt be saved."[1] This is the way, and the truth, and the life. My dear child, what should, what could we lost sinners do, if it were not for this atoning merit? Seek, and you shall find. Lose no time. Christ waits to be gracious; carry your heart and all its feelings to him in prayer, and when you have told him all your wants, pray for your affectionate father,

L. RICHMOND

*Note to his second Daughter.*

MY DEAREST FANNY—As I trust it is your own and my wish, that your mind should be seriously and affectionately directed towards the greatest of all external privileges, the Lord's supper, I wish you to answer me in writing, these two questions: What are your views of the nature, design, and privilege of this sacrament? and what are the real feelings of your heart at this time respecting it? This communication is, and shall be, quite confidential between you and your affectionate

FATHER

P. S.—I trust the first Saturday in October may unite us at the feast of love.

*To his second Son.*

AROS, AUGUST 14, 1820

MY DEAR WILBERFORCE—How little idea can my son form of the scenes with which his father is surrounded, amongst these highlands and islands of the north. It is like being in another world. In some of these remote islands, where the Gaelic language is chiefly spoken—though not to the exclusion of the English—where different manners, dress, habits, dwellings, etc., prevail,

"The world forgetting, by the world forgot"[2]

_____

1 Acts 16:31.
2 A quote from *Eloisa to Abelard* by Alexander Pope.

it seems difficult to conceive that it is still Britain. I am now on my way for Staffa and Iona, but whether the weather will be fine enough to allow of my projected excursion, remains a doubt; you shall know before this letter is concluded. I propose this evening to gather a little company of highland cotters, and to preach to them in a wild glen, in this romantic island. The parish church is fifteen miles distant. Yesterday I came from Oban, which is thirty-five miles by sea from this place; but owing to the wind being in the wrong direction, we made tacks amounting to one hundred miles, before we got into this little peaceful spot. This is a little inn: before it, in one direction, is the sea, and beyond, a vast range of mountains, called Morven, in Argyleshire; in another direction, about half a mile off, is a ruined castle, standing on a bold knoll and rock, washed by the waves. On our right hand are the hills of the Isle of Mull, covered with heath and cottages. Before the door runs a salmon stream, rattling over stones: above thirty people were yesterday fishing and harpooning for salmon; fifty of them weighed from four to twenty-five pounds each. Dozens of children were in the river to catch eels, talking Gaelic with much vocifera-tion and alacrity.

I think, in our voyage yesterday, I saw twenty ruined castles, and three inhabited ones, and above twenty-five of the islands of the Hebrides. The intelligent boatmen tell you all manner of ancient legends and histories connected with them and their ancient mas-ters. They carry you back into the days of Norwegian, Danish, and Irish story. I saw the spot where a part of the Spanish armada was wrecked; and a gun still remains on a rock, belonging to one of the Spanish ships. It is on the mainland shore, opposite to the Isle of Mull. This is the grand scene of all Ossian's descriptions, and cor-responds exactly with them. All the ruins are finely covered with ivy, and so are the rocks.

We have had much rain, and the mountain-torrents run grandly down their sides. I think on Thursday we counted three hundred and fifty cascades, in a morning ride; some of them gigantic.

I remember seeing twenty-nine at one view. The wild magnificence of highland scenery cannot easily be conceived. Parties of ladies are amongst the visitants, and in some places they cheerfully submit to many privations for the sake of the prospect. I go into the cottages, and sit down with the poor people, and talk with them on religious subjects, and receive rich milk in return. There is much grateful affection about them.

I am very thankful to God for permitting me to take this round, and more so for making my services very acceptable, and I hope useful. The tempest-beaten glens, the secluded isles, the populous towns, the romantic villages, all in their turn bear witness to the declaration of "the truth as it is in Jesus." I have a truly congenial companion in the "Clemens" of the Christian Guardian;[1] he is just what I want, both for soul and body, and in each devotes himself to my aid and comfort most assiduously. Our views, principles, taste, and feelings, strictly accord. He is a student of divinity in the university at Edinburgh, and preparing for the Scotch church. I left Mary with Dr. S., last Tuesday; she will soon go to Edinburgh, and wait till my return from the north of Scotland. I shall now lay down my pen, and probably not resume it until the point is decided, tomorrow or next day, whether the rain will allow of our visiting these most interesting of islands, Staffa and Iona. The latter is thirty miles from hence; the former twenty, but on the opposite side.

TUESDAY, Aug. 15. Very wet, and we cannot proceed. Both Iona, at twenty, and Staffa, at ten miles distance, are in sight, but it is very doubtful whether we shall reach them, as the Atlantic is full of mists, rain, and wind. I am waiting patiently for better weather, in a little inn, in this little island, five miles by three.

—— 18. My dear boy, I have seen Staffa, and write this from Iona. What I shall say I know not, for really I can say nothing as I ought. When I entered the cave of Fingal, I knew not whether to burst out into one unceasing cry of astonishment, or meditate in unbroken silence of overwhelming wonder, or fall down upon

1 The Rev. D. Pitcairn. *(Original footnote)*

my knees in devout adoration of Him who formed such a scene of sublime beauty. It beggars all description. This was on Wednesday: after waiting four days for weather, yesterday we arrived at this lonely scene of ruins and curiosities, and it more than answers all my expectations. Think of all we have read about Iona, and imagine then a small part of my sensations.

My dear Boy— . . . It is high time that you and I should communicate frequently, intimately, and confidentially. If this is not to be expected by the time you have arrived at fifteen, when is it to be looked for? On one account, I have more solicitude, and even dread, on your behalf, than for any of my children. Earnestly as I should wish a son of mine to be a minister, yet I tremble at the idea of educating and devoting a son to the sacred profession, without a previous satisfactory evidence that his own soul is right with God. Without this, you and I should be guilty of a most awful sin in his sight. To any, and every other good profession, trade, or occupation, it may be lawful and expedient to fix with some degree of determination, long before entering upon it; but the ministry is an exception. Even St. Paul himself trembles at his responsibility, and exclaims, "lest, when I have preached to others, I myself should be a castaway."[1] I consider personal religion, accompanied and evidenced by personal conduct, to be indispensable in the individual, before either he, or another for him, fixes on the ministry for his profession. And I will not hesitate to say to *you*, that, honored and happy as I should feel, in being permitted to see you a faithful preacher of righteousness, adorning the Gospel which you would proclaim to others; yet without this, I would rather a thousand times see you a mason, or in the humblest capacity in life. I know what the office is; and a penitent sense of my own deficiencies teaches me to be fearful, and to tremble for those of others: how much more so in the case of my own child?

The national church groans and bleeds, "from the crown of its

---

1  1 Corinthians 9:27.

head to the sole of its feet," through the daily intrusion of unworthy men into its ministry. Patrons, parents, tutors, colleges, are annually pouring a torrent of incompetent youths into the church, and loading the nation with spiritual guilt. Hence, souls are neglected and ruined—bigotry and ignorance prevail—church pride triumphs over church godliness—and the establishment is despised, deserted, and wounded. Shall you and I deepen these wounds? shall we add one more unit to the numbers of the unworthy and traitorous watchmen on the towers of our British Jerusalem? God forbid! But to avoid so sad a departure from every principle of sacred order and conscience, *you* must become a humble, seriously-minded, consistent young disciple of Christ; a diligent student, an obedient son, a loving brother, a grateful worshipper, a simple-hearted Christian. And *I* must feel comfortably satisfied that you are so: or with what conscience, with what hope, with what satisfaction, with what peace of mind, can I consent to devote you to the most sacred, the most important, the most responsible of all offices within the compass of human existence?

Now, I will not, and ought not to conceal from you, that, however accustomed we may all have been to talk of you as a future clergyman, I dare not decide upon any such plan without a much more clear evidence than I have yet seen, that your actual state of feelings and conduct, temper and conversation, habitual and permanent thoughts, are such as will justify me in coming to so solemn a determination on my own part.

I say this with anxiety, and write it with fear, as my pen proceeds; but I say it with earnest prayers for the real conversion of your soul to God, and with some hope that he will hear the petitions which I have offered up for you through many a long year. I still repeat it, that I never can consent to put my seal to the question of the ministry, unless, and until I have some satisfactory proof of your heart being turned to God, in holy consistency and permanence of character.

Let these pages be a testimony before God, and keep them as a sign between you and me, that I am in earnest as to a subject where indifference would be sin.

I have long been studying your character in the hourly events of each day, in immediate reference to this point. . . . Remember, "they that are Christ's have crucified the flesh, with its affections and lusts":[1] crucify yours. Pursue your studies with diligence: you may do great things for yourself, even without help; although, I grant, much better with it. But "work while it is day; the night cometh, when no man can work."[2]

Believe me your affectionate father,

L. R.

*To his second Daughter.*

MY DEAR LOVE—Was not this the day on which you were born? Why, then, I must now wish you many happy returns of it. But will they be happy, if you be not holy? How I long to see my dear Fanny still more decided, more spiritual, more given to holy thoughts, words, and works. Let not your mind be drawn aside by any thing that will steal your heart from God. Make no idols of books that carry away the imagination. I will give you a rule to judge whether an author is profitable in the perusal. Go directly from your book, and open your Bible; and, without partiality or hypocrisy, say which you embrace with the most delight. The answer will always show the state of your mind, and the profitableness and lawfulness of the book.

Become more serious. I am much pleased with the conscientious principles and behavior of Mary and Mr. M., in their intercourse. He is a true Christian, and most affectionately attached to her. His views of faith and practice exactly accord with my own; he is too good a man to be light and trifling on such a solemn subject as a nuptial engagement. Mary's mind is sacredly and steadfastly made up, to love, honor, and obey him, as the partner of her heart,

---

1 Galatians 5:24.
2 John 9:4.

and the choice of her conscience. Oh, pray for the dear girl, and treat the question with sacred cheerfulness. My visit to Glasgow was blessed to the cultivation of pure regard and esteem with *all* the M——s. I can resign her, with full hope and confidence, into God's hands. Do you the same; and when we return home, seek more opportunities of useful conversation. Attend, in the course of every day and hour, to the growth of your best and most ennobling principles of action. Much, very much time, which might be employed in an increasing meetness for the inheritance of the saints in light, is, I fear, lost. These things ought not so to be, my dear child. Time is short, eternity is at hand. It is a hard thing to be saved at all; and every lost hour, every idle word, every neglected opportunity, makes it more hard. It is a strait gate and narrow way to heaven, and, comparatively, few there be that find it.

Never be without a book, in daily reading, *of a direct spiritual and devotional tendency;* one that will make the vanities of time and sense appear unworthy of your notice. Always maintain with some one, if possible, a truly religious correspondence, calculated to bring Christ to the soul. Keep in hourly recollection that you are a great sinner, unworthy of all the comforts and enjoyments which you possess; and that without a Saviour inwardly known, all is as nothing. Examine for the proofs of a converted mind, in the grand act of faith on Jesus Christ. I cannot recommend you a more lively example than Mrs. Isabella Graham, the admirable aunt of Mr. M. Learn to love true religion in others, whoever they may be. Shun party prejudice, as the bane of charity and the curse of the church. God's love is not limited to us, and our division of the church of Christ; why then ought ours? Far be it from us to feel alienation from any whom he is leading heavenwards.

Pray think of the general tenor of this letter, for my sake, and for your own sake. I have much spiritual uneasiness about all my children, and most anxiously wish to see them grow in grace. Without this, all is dead. I want to see them useful to others around them, and patterns to one another, and comforts to me in all things.

*To the same.*

SEA BANK, AYRSHIRE

MY MUCH-LOVED FANNY—As you hear all the good news from Glasgow, I need not repeat it. Now take a Scotch map, and you shall see where I am. Look on the sea-coast of Ayrshire, and you see a place between Ayr and Largs, called Salt Coasts. Close to this is a lovely cottage called Sea Bank, the residence of my friend Mr. ——. In the front is a magnificent view of the sea as far as Ireland—the Frith of Clyde with its beauteous islands—Arran, whose craggy picturesque mountains tower to the sky in the wildest, highest style of romantic grandeur and beauty—Bute, smaller, but very lovely— the Cumbraies—the long peninsula of Cantyre, and over it the high pyramidical mountains of Jura—the coast of Ayrshire, farther than the eye can reach, and the surprising rock called the Craig of Ailsa, rising up in the midst of the ocean, far away from all land, and sustaining solitary majesty, the almost unmolested haunt of wild birds, goats, and rabbits. Yesterday there was a great storm, and the sea raged horribly. I saw many a vessel tossed about in all directions. I went down to the shore, and stood astounded amidst roaring waves, screaming sea-fowls, and whistling winds. Today all is calm, gentle, and inviting. Yesterday I saw the sublime, today the beautiful. I am writing at a window which commands the whole view. Somehow or other I am much amused with the appearance and conduct of a large flock of poultry, just now parading about on the lawn beneath me. There are five pea-fowls, six turkeys, twenty cocks and hens, and a solitary goose from Botany Bay. They walk and talk with much diversified gait and air. The sober gravity of their pace, occasionally interrupted by a gobble, a jump, and a snap; the proud loftiness of the peacock, sometimes expressed in solemn silence, and sometimes by a very unmusical squall. The ruffling vibrations of the turkeycock's feathers, with now and then a brisk advance towards his rival on the green; the social grouping of the cocks and hens, contrasted with the unsocial condition and march of the poor unpartnered goose, who grunts dismally, and sometimes turns up a doubtful sort of a sidelook at me, as I sit at the window, as much as to say, "Who are you?" Sometimes a continued silence for a space, and then a sudden and universal cackling, as if they were all at once tickled or frightened, or in some way excited to garrulity. All this amuses me not a little. There are also two noble watch-dogs; I wish they had been at the house when the robbers came. I feel much when at a distance from home; even minor sources of trouble harass and disturb me, when I am so far from you. Let us pray for faith and confidence in God alone. I think of going to Iona; it is sacred and classic ground. May every blessing attend my children.

So prays their affectionate father,

LEGH RICHMOND

*To the same.*

GLASGOW

MY OWN DEAR CHILD—On my return home, I found your letter, and hasten to give you a few lines in reply. I thought you long in writing, and welcomed your hand with much delight. Indeed, my Fanny, you and I are not sufficiently intimate in religious inter-course and correspondence; we must become more so, and may God enable us. Let us walk and talk, and sit and talk more on these subjects than we have done. Time flies, events are uncertain, provi-dences, health, and life are transient and mutable. I hope the ensu-ing winter will unite us closer than ever. Winter is my domestic dependence; your heart is with me in this feeling. I much regret that circumstances have prevented your travelling with me this year, but I hope next summer will be more propitious. When I return, we will read and talk over together such scenes as we mutually love, and you shall hear of my interesting journey to Staffa and Iona. Nature, grace, history, antiquity, compassion, taste, and twenty more sub-jects and affections all meet there. I will match the festival which I gave to the poor children of Icolmkill on St. Colomba's day with the gala of Mr. ——. Moreover I wrote a right noble copy of verses for the children to sing. Mr. M. is a truly valuable man. He grows daily in my estimation. I feel much pleased at the prospect of my dear Mary's union; her tender heart is fixed, although her affections are strongly bound to her family. Encourage and elevate her spirits when you write, for her nerves are delicate. It is a great question, and God, I trust, is settling it for her. . . . Mr. M. is a man of God, and makes religion and conscience the ground of all he says and does.

Read the life of Mrs. Isabella Graham of New York, Mr. M.'s aunt. It will show you the sort of piety of Mr. M. and his family, all of whom are valuable characters.

What a terrible storm you had. The Lord rides in the storm. "He can create, and he destroy." I hope you do not forget him in the midst of agreeable society. The care of a soul, its natural departures from God, its proneness to make idols of the creature, and the extreme narrowness of the strait gate, are subjects for our deep meditation. Alas, how many among our respectable and decent friends and acquaintance are still in an unconverted state, strangers to the real experience of the heart, and unacquainted with the love of Christ. Carelessness and comparative insensibility, ruin more souls than deliberate acts of resolute iniquity. You have need to be jealous over your own soul, and to watch and pray that you enter not into temptation. *Real* piety is a very different thing from mere decent profession, educational propriety, and orderly conduct; yet without it none can enter the kingdom of God. Where a deep sense of guilt and depravity does not subsist, all else is a mere name; and it is much easier to admit this as a doctrine, than to feel and act upon it as a truth. I want my children to be living commentaries on my sermons and principles. I long to see them *adorning* the Gospel of Christ in all things, and that from the inner man of the heart. I have no objection to Mr. ——'s being liberal and hospitable. I only lament that among the lower classes, dancing and debauchery are nearly synonymous, and therefore I must absent myself from such fêtes. So poor dear S. W.[1] is dead. To what trials are the best

1 One of his poor parishioners. (*Original footnote*)

Christians for a time given up. Frequently, during delirium, the most holy have appeared the most wicked in thought and action. But of *her* Christianity I cannot have a doubt. . . . I saw —— last week. . . . Oh, how time flies; generation succeeds generation, like waves on the sea; but whither shall *we* float at last? Much, much, very much goes to secure a safe entrance into the eternal harbor of peace and safety. All subjects sink into insignificance compared with this. How foolish, how wicked are we in this matter. Farewell, my beloved Fanny; much of my domestic comfort depends on you; love your father, for indeed he loves you. When and while you can, be a prop to his feelings and spirits. Now the period is arrived when I look for the harvest of filial intercourse, of which I sowed the seeds with such anxiety in your infancy and childhood. May every blessing be with you, in time and eternity. Seven times a day I pray, and say, "God bless my dear wife; God bless my dear children; God bless my dear parishioners; and God bless my own immortal soul."

This comes from the heart of

Your loving father,

LEGH RICHMOND

*To the same.*

One thing, my Fanny, is most certain, that a great deal more than commonly manifests itself amongst the generality of rich and genteel professors, is necessary to adorn, if not constitute, real, vital, saving religion. The manners, the opinions, the luxuries, the indolence, the trifling, the waste of time and talents, the low standard, the fastidiousness, the pride, and many more etceteras stand awfully in the way of religious attainment and progress; hence it is, that in so many instances, the religion of the cottage so much outstrips that of the mansion, and that we derive so much more benefit from intercourse with the really sincere Christians amongst the poor, than amongst the too refined, showy, luxurious, and dubious professors in higher classes. Thank God, however, there are some, though few, yet delightful specimens amongst the rich;

the gate is too strait for some of the camels. . . . Allow me, with a heart full of love and esteem for my dearly-loved Fanny, to ask whether you have considered the subject of my last letter? Do you not see, on mature examination of your own heart, that religion has not done all that it ought to have done in this respect for my dearest child? Has not something of discontent been mingled with the lawful exercise of affection? Has not Christ been in some degree robbed of his love and duty in your heart of late? I entreat my dear child to take this frank but affectionate reproof in good part. I love you so dearly, that I want to see you holy, happy, and heavenly. True, deep, and unfeigned piety will alone induce a right frame; not the fretful weariedness of this world, but the mind reconciled to all the dealings of the Lord, because they are *his*, and that for both worlds. I gave an historical, antiquarian, ecclesiastical, picturesque, mineralogical, and religious lecture on Iona and Staffa, to about one hundred and fifty ladies and gentlemen in the schoolroom at Olney last Wednesday. I spoke for two hours and a half. I produced fifty illustrative pictures, and all my pebbles and other specimens. I did the same at Embarton. All expressed satisfaction.

Your affectionate father,

L. R.

# Chapter 3

## LETTER TO HIS DAUGHTER MARY, ON THE DAY OF HER MARRIAGE—LETTERS TO WILBERFORCE, WHILE IN DECLINING HEALTH—LETTERS TO HIS SECOND DAUGHTER

The great solemnity with which Mr. Richmond regarded the assumption of the duties of married life by a young female, has been already seen by frequent allusions in preceding letters. But the following specific directions to his daughter, on an occasion of this kind, make us better acquainted with his feelings in relation to it.

*To his eldest Daughter, on the day of her marriage.*

I this day consign you, my beloved daughter, into the hands of one whom I believe to be a man of God, and who will watch over your eternal as well as your temporal interests. I trust that your union is formed in the simplicity of faith, hope, and love. Give yourself up, first to God, and then to your husband, for Christ's sake. Pray for grace to conduct yourself aright, in the new stations of wife and mistress. Never depend, for a single moment, on the strength of your own feeble nature. Live constantly by faith on the Son of God; relying on him for the graces of domestic life, as well as those of a more general character. Endeavor in all things to please God, and you will be sure to please all whom you ought to please.

Expect the trials and crosses incident to the earthly pilgrimage; but expect also, by the mercies and merits of Jesus Christ, to be enabled to pass through them with safety and peace.

Love, honor, and obey your husband, for the Lord's sake. Do it upon deep conscientious principles, as in the constant sight of God. Think much on the love of Christ to poor sinners; and live upon this love, as food and medicine to your own soul.

Be cheerful without levity; be grave without moroseness; be devout without affectation; be firm without obstinacy; be diligent in business, fervent in spirit, serving the Lord in all things.

Although you leave your father's house, I know you will not leave its principles, any more than its love. Though separated, we shall be closely united; though out of sight, yet never out of mind; you will think of us, and we of you, with affections tender, rational, and abiding. We shall often meet at the throne of grace, and welcome each other, and be welcome there; we shall often meet in the correspondences of heart and pen. We shall, if God permit, sometimes meet in sweet personal intercourse again; we shall often meet in the affectionate reveries of imagination. And oh, may we at last meet to part no more, in the house not made with hands, eternal in the heavens.

Study your own and your husband's dispositions, that you may cultivate true conjugal peace and love. Ever be ready to open your heart to him on things spiritual as well as temporal. Disappoint him not herein, for he will watch over your soul as one that must give account. A minister's public labors are intimately connected with his private and domestic consolations. A minister's wife may be a mainspring of encouragement or discouragement to her husband, in all his arduous and anxious occupations for the good of his flock. On her example and demeanor very much may often depend. Keep this always in mind, and look up to Christ for gracious help. Feel with and for your husband, in all his parochial and congregational interests, as well as in those which are simply domestic—they ought to be inseparable. Cultivate a deep and personal piety. Imitate the holy women of old, and let your adorning be like unto theirs: St. Peter can tell you what that is. 1 PETER, 3:3–5.[1]

---

1 1 Peter 3:3–5—[3]Whose adorning let it not be that outward adorning of plaiting the hair, and of wearing of gold, or of putting on of apparel; [4]But let it be the hidden man of the heart, in that which is not corruptible, even the ornament

I rejoice in your lot; I can see the hand of God in it. This is a token for good to us all.

Go, dear Mary, to your husband's house; and may the presence and blessing of the Lord go with you: I commend you to his holy keeping, with confidence. Faithful is He that hath promised, and he will do it. We shall have pledged our vows at the table of the Lord, at this interesting period; may this strengthen and animate our hearts to serve and trust him. On this day the Spirit was poured out on the primitive church with great power: may we this day receive the earnest of his love in much simplicity.

Grace, peace, and mercy, be with my beloved daughter, and with her affectionate father,

LEGH RICHMOND

*To the same, on his own birthday.*

MY VERY DEAR DAUGHTER—Through many a returning year, I wrote to my dear and venerated mother on my birthday. She is gone to her rest, and I can only communicate with her in grateful recollection and hopeful anticipation. To whom can I now address myself with more propriety and love, on such an occasion, than to my absent, distant but much-loved child? My child, so mercifully restored to health after so severe an illness and so much danger, my thoughts and prayers have been unceasing respecting you. I have endeavored patiently to wait upon the Lord, and he hath heard my prayer. I have viewed this trying dispensation as sent of God for some great and good purpose, to your own and to all our souls; and I trust we shall find it so. You will have to learn to glorify God in the fires,[1] and magnify the God of your salvation; to see the precarious tenure of human life, and to devote your restored powers of mind and body to him from whom you have received both. O, my dear Mary, what a God he is, and what a redemption

---

of a meek and quiet spirit, which is in the sight of God of great price. [5]For after this manner in the old time the holy women also, who trusted in God, adorned themselves, being in subjection unto their own husbands.

1 Mrs. M. had been suffering from an accident by fire. *(Original footnote)*

he has wrought for sinners. See in your own recent trial an emblem of Christ's love; yourself a brand plucked from the burning; saved, yet so as by fire: raised from weakness to strength; tempest-tossed and afflicted, yet preserved; cast down, but not destroyed. It is the heart's desire and prayer to God of your father, on his birthday, that all these things may work together for your good, temporal and spiritual. It is a day which I always contemplate with much tender affection, and my thoughts are such as I cannot utter. Life, death, and eternity spread a vision before me, and I meditate with solemnity and deep humiliation. I have lived now more than half a century. On the past I look with much repentance for my sins, and much gratitude for my mercies. Of the future I know nothing, except that my times are in God's hands, and that is enough. But my responsibilities make me often tremble. They rise like mountains before me; but I lift up my eyes to the hills from whence cometh my help, and the mountains of difficulty become plains, and the rough places smooth. Amongst my mercies I feel peculiarly thankful for the union of my dear child with such a man and such a minister as Mr. M——. This doubly endears Scotland to my heart. I have formed many valuable friendships, and received many kind favors from its inhabitants. I have delighted in its scenery, and tasted many excellent fruits of its piety: but to have a daughter placed in the midst of Scotia's hills and plains, renders the land peculiarly interesting to me.

May every day add to your strength and comfort. May you and I, not only as parent and child, but as fellow-pilgrims on the road to Zion, walk lovingly, congenially, and safely to the end of our journey. I hope, if God spare me, to see you in the spring; but whether here or there, I am ever

Your affectionate father,

L. R.

*To the same.*

DEAR MARY—I wrote to you on my *own* birthday, and now I do

the same on *yours*. "There is a time to be born, and a time to die."[1] So says Solomon; and it is the memento of a truly wise man. But I may add, there is an interval between these two *times*, of infinite importance.

Does my beloved child duly appreciate this? Not all the charms of nature, either Scottish or English, can for a moment compare with those of grace: and when can we better contemplate the real value of life, the vanity of the world, the worth of a soul, and the need of a Saviour, than when the lapse of time brings round the anniversary day of our birth? It seems to concentrate all the experience and feeling of past days, and to unite them with the anticipation of those which are yet to come; it speaks to youth and age alike, and summons both to prayer and meditation. Soon will eternity overwhelm all the concerns of time, but will infallibly take its character *from* them. I sincerely hope that you are systematically improving time, with a view to *that* eternity. Your opportunities have been many and valuable, your privileges great—may every ensuing day prove that they are not lost upon you. Religious parentage and social connections alone cannot save; personal religion in the heart is every thing. Our dear friend Mrs. S—— appears to enjoy it in deed and in truth. Prize such a friend; not only because she is kind, and agreeable, and worthy, but because she is a child of God, a member of Christ, and an inheritor of the kingdom of heaven; and *as such*, may be the ordained instrument of God for establishing the same principle in you. Think of us all, not for the mere love's sake of earthly kindred, but for the love of Jesus, as connected with the family of heaven. This alone gives to charity itself its value.

Farewell, my dear child; and while you pray for yourself, forget not
Your affectionate father,

LEGH RICHMOND

*To his second Daughter.*

LONDON, JUNE 7, 1822

Fully as I can enter into the beauties of works of fiction, yet I

---

1 Ecclesiastes 3:2.

exceedingly dread their tendency. The utmost caution is requisite in meddling with them. The novelist I unequivocally proscribe, and many of the poets, and their poems, which are only nets to catch young minds in the maze of Satan. It is a maxim in regard to books, as well as companions, that what does not *improve,* invariably *injures.* Few things in this world are merely negative and harmless: they either do us good, when, sanctified by the Spirit, or they do us harm by stealing our hearts from God. Even the beauties and wonders of nature, in an unsanctified mind, excite nothing beyond natural affections—pleasure and surprise. If *Christ* is not sought for in them, we rise no higher than mere tourists, rhymists, and painters. Whether we eat, or drink, or travel, or read, or converse, or philosophize—all, *all must be done to the glory of God.*

The health of his son Wilberforce having become such as to occasion solicitude, he visited Scotland, where the three following letters were addressed to him.

TURVEY, JUNE 12, 1824

MY DEAR BOY—I have, as I mentioned to you the other day, for some time wished to press upon your attention the important subject of the Lord's supper; and, as in the case of each of your sisters, I found that some epistolary correspondence afforded a liberty and facility of communication in the first instance, I trust you will not object to adopting a similar mode. A time of relaxation from your studies, and of indisposition, may afford you good opportunity for such a purpose. It will be exceedingly gratifying to me to receive some simple, faithful account of your state of mind, views, feelings, and desires, in connection with the privilege and duty of commemorating the dying love of Christ to sinners. I wish to receive you at the table of our Lord, both as your affectionate father in the flesh, and your still happier father in the Spirit, with principles enlightened, and heart warmed with a Saviour's mercies. Approach me thus, my beloved son, and write to me with a free, confidential heart. I feel the most lively interest in your spiritual welfare, far beyond what my

ordinary manner may betray. You are arrived at an age, when I wish
you to become my bosom friend and companion in all things, but
above all, in those things which belong to our everlasting peace. I
have sometimes feared that other subjects have somewhat monopo-
lized your thoughts; and yet I have the firmest hope that your mind
is truly sensible of the value and importance of divine things. I trust
you are constant in prayer, and that your affections are unfeignedly
directed towards divine truth. I cannot express to you how much
this belief comforts and strengthens my mind. It is allied to every
feeling and wish which I have so long and so anxiously cherished,
in regard to your future character, as a minister of the gospel of
Christ. None but God knows how intense my solicitude has been
upon that point. It is high time that you should, by the open act
of communion, devote yourself to the Redeemer's service, and look
upon it as a pledge for your inward principles and outward practice.
You should . . . always have a book of experimental and devotional
character, more or less in private reading. It must ever be kept in
remembrance, that the mere literary, discussional study of theology,
however valuable and needful, is a distinct thing from the affectionate work of the heart in the exercises of the conscience in the soul.
I am earnest that my dear child should enjoy all the privileges of
the church of Christ, and adorn them. Search for the evidences of
a renewed heart daily; come as a lost, undone sinner, and may you
taste that the Lord is gracious. Beware of the world's temptations
and levities. We should all feel that time is short, and eternity at
hand, and be prepared accordingly. The regular partaking of the
Lord's supper, when rightly viewed, has a tendency to cherish the
best affections of the soul, and to preserve both young and old from
the dangerous delusions of the world, the flesh, and Satan. Let the
communication of these thoughts excite you to self-examination,
meditation, and prayer. My love and regard for you are great indeed;
my own heart is wrapped up in the prosperity of yours. May all your
studies be sanctified to the glory of God. May you *now* enjoy a portion of those pleasures which are at God's right hand for evermore.

"The blood of Christ cleanseth from all sin."[1] How delightful a thought for you and for

Your affectionate father,

LEGH RICHMOND

TURVEY, JUNE 22, 1824

MY VERY DEAR CHILD—I present you with this book, for the express purpose of your keeping a journal and diary, not merely of passing events, as they may occur, but of the thoughts of your heart upon divine things. I earnestly entreat you to do this; I recommend it from long experience, as a most beneficial exercise. It is perfectly secret to yourself and God. No one can ever see it without your own knowledge and consent. But such records have been so useful, so consolatory, and so improving, that I make it my paternal entreaty that you will comply with this request. Suspended in uncertainty with regard to your health and strength, my soul is most anxious for your spiritual good. Trifle not, delay not in this matter. Press forward to the mark and prize of your high calling. Review the past thoughts of your heart—examine the present—anticipate the future. You are in God's hands. I trust the everlasting arms are underneath you. Let me entreat you to open your mind also to me, in frequent correspondence. I cannot express my solicitude for your spiritual welfare. You know all the principles by which a sinner may be saved: you have known them from your infancy: may they be the ornament of your youth. Rest short of nothing but a well-grounded conviction of your personal interest in Christ. There is a rich provision in him for every possible difficulty and deficiency which can present itself to your thoughts. Oh, how does my heart burn to see you, in every sense of the word, a true Christian. In a former note I invited you to the Lord's table. Happy, thrice happy shall I be, to see you there, added to the number of the Lord's flock.

Since writing the above, I have received yours. I thank you from my heart. Go on, as your strength and opportunities will allow, by

---

1  1 John 1:7.

a little at a time; but give me as much of your thoughts and feel-ings as you can. Tell me of your past years, and early leadings and convictions; tell me more of those things which you have named in former letters. You cannot oblige me more, than by giving me the *history* of your heart at various periods. I have known too little of you, my dear child. Let that ignorance on my part cease. I have loved you from your birth, and watched over you till now, with the tenderest affections, but I feel my own deficiency in not commun-ing more with you on the state of your mind in the sight of God. Comfort me now by *frequent* intercourse on these matters. It is the very return of all others which I desire for all the past anxieties of a father and a minister. May this journey be blessed to you both in soul and body. I trust soon, with God's blessing, to see you again. In the meantime, I commend you to Him who has all events in his hands, whose consolations are neither few nor small, who gave his Son to die for your sins, and whose compassions fail not. Be much in prayer and self-examination. The God of the waves shall protect and guard you; the God of the land shall comfort you. But seek him aright; trifle not with the great concern. How joyfully shall I wel-come you at the Lord's table, if God so will. Adieu for the present, my child, my friend, and, in Christ, my brother.

LEGH RICHMOND

TURVEY, JUNE 30, 1824

MY EVER-DEAR SON—I thank you for your letter, and am glad to hear again from Mr. Marshall that you have borne your travels so far well. You are never out of my thoughts, and I follow you in imagination through every scene of your occupation. But there is an eye that beholds and watches over you, in a way that I cannot do. To Him I confide and commend you, for sickness and health, for time and eternity. What a word, what a thought is eternity. What prospects does it set before us. What inconceivable myster-ies are involved in it. How does it make the things of time dwindle into insignificance. But what questions of unspeakable import are involved in it. Sin, corrupt nature, a broken law, an offended God, eternal punishment; conscience, guilt, regeneration, salvation by Christ; faith, hope, love, free-grace, undeserved mercy, justification, effectual calling, adoption into God's family, pardon of sin, consolation in Christ, heaven and glory. These, and a thousand accompaniments, are all connected with the idea, and the reality of eternity. What a sad proof of the depravity of our hearts is our indifference towards thinking, and our backwardness towards speaking upon those things which belong to our everlasting peace; and which, nevertheless, if neglected, involve our eternal ruin. We need warnings, and the Lord sends them in many ways. Sickness, pain, bereavements, losses, disappointments, all bring their message with them. The great question between a soul and God is not whether we admit the truths of the Scripture into our understandings, but *whether they are so applied to our hearts as to have wrought a change, and become vital principles of faith and practice.* Nothing short of this can afford evidence of a saved and safe condition. There is an action of the soul by which it rests upon Christ, and all that he has done, with full confidence; and this produces peace in the conscience. The more we see of ourselves, the more we see our sin; and the more we see our sin, the more we fly to the death and righteousness of Christ, for pardon, deliverance, and hope. We behold not only his sufficiency, but his willingness to save the chief of sinners. For this we love him; and if we love him, we desire and endeavor to keep his commandments; and this is the way of salvation.

Now, does my dear boy view this in all its integrity? Do the experiences of the past, strengthened by all the variety and succession of instruction which you have from your infancy received, work together to this great end? Can you be satisfied with any thing short of this? God forbid. Let nothing interrupt you in this continual work of self-examination; and let self-examination lead you to earnest and ardent prayer. Let no pursuits of literature, no delights of sense, no passing occurrences, no debility of body, no inferior subjects of recreation, prevent you from keeping your thoughts close to God and to eternity. Great have been your mercies, may your gratitude be great likewise.

Accustomed as I am to close and faithful dealings with my Christian friends and flock, it would ill become me to be silent or indifferent where my dearly beloved child is concerned. Sickness gives both you and me a wholesome admonition. I pray God, from the depths of my heart, that we may each of us improve it to our spiritual welfare. God may have great things to accomplish hereby: let us believe and hope so.

I had much pleasure in showing you London; and if Providence permit, may yet have more, in viewing the fine scenery in your present vicinity, along with you: but whether amongst the beauties of art or nature, never, never cease to look for and contemplate the God both of creation and redemption in the midst of all. Keep a continual watch over your disposition, temper, and thoughts. There are not only sins of the temper, but of the understanding also; and pride in every form, intellectual as well as sensual, must be brought low. "Learn of me," said the Saviour, "for I am meek and lowly of heart."[1] I write, as I would talk with and pray for you. May this dispensation of the Almighty, which has for the present separated us, and given us cause for much anxiety on your account, be a season of much profit to us all. Lay these things to heart, make them the subject of unceasing petition at that throne whence no believing supplicants are ever sent empty away. Wonder not that I cannot rest contented with a superficial religion, but that I look for a deeply experimental life of God in your soul. I place time and eternity before me in holy imagination. I strive, as it were, to penetrate the veil which separates them, and to look earnestly at those things which belong to your and my everlasting peace. Forgive me, my dear child, and may God forgive me, if I have not always and equally pressed these subjects upon your personal attention. They have ever lain near to my heart, and you have had multiplied opportunities of meditating upon them. I trust you have done so. But let me know more and

1 Matthew 11:29.

more of your thoughts, past and present. My Christian and parental peace is dependent greatly upon it. I am glad that our friend Dr. Stewart has had so good an opportunity of studying your case. You are in the Lord's hands. May he overrule every thing for your good. May our confidence be placed only where it is due; and pray for your father, and your father shall pray for you. Amongst the books in your travelling library, are many most valuable authors. Read, mark, learn, and inwardly digest what they say, so far as you find time and strength to peruse them. Above all, search the Scriptures, for in them you have eternal life. Your mother sends her entire and most affectionate love to you: your sisters and brothers the same. And what shall I add for myself? All that is tender, affectionate, parental, and Christian,

From your father,

L. R.

In the month of July, Mr. Richmond joined his son in Scotland, using every means for the restoration of his health. During a short interval of separation, he addressed to him another letter, expressive of the same ardent desire for his spiritual welfare, and written in the same delightful strain of warm and affectionate feeling.

BRADFORD, AUGUST 5, 1824

MY DEAR WILBERFORCE—We have so long been fellow-travellers and pilgrims together, and my eye and my heart have been so long accustomed to watch over you, that I cannot help wishing to indulge my affectionate feelings, by giving you a few lines during this short separation, which, short as it has been, never ceases to present my dear boy to imagination and recollection. I have reason to think, and perhaps the fault is my own, that you are but *imperfectly* aware of my strong and anxious feeling towards you, with respect both to your temporal and spiritual welfare. I sometimes fancy I see this in your manner, and it hurts me. I say little, or probably nothing; but my heart is alive to great sensibilities. Rest assured, my much-loved child, that at all past periods, but most especially since it has pleased God to put your health, and of course with it your life, to so marked a trial, I have not ceased for a single hour—and I can hardly except the dreaming hours of the night—to make *your* comfort and prosperity the subject of my prayers and solicitude. When you may least have suspected it from my ordinary manner, even my silence has spoken to God in your behalf. Many and deep have been my meditations, as we ascended the hills, and descended the vales of Scotland; or as we ploughed the waters with our prows and paddles. I have often experienced a kind of stupid impotency of utterance, when my heart has been animated and full. You likewise manifest a sort of reserve on the subject of personal religion, which checks, and sometimes chills my rising inclination to more unreserved, free, congenial, and comfortable conversation. I wish all this to vanish; and that whatever may be the will of God concerning you, the future days which his providence may permit us mutually to spend together, may be more distinctly marked by free and affectionate communications. But far, far above all, it is my cherished and anxious hope, that you may evince an increasing love to spiritual things, to reading, conversing, and meditating upon the things which belong to your everlasting peace. You have had your warning as to the delicate and precarious tenure by which life, health, and youthful vigor are held. Every day and hour still reminds you of the uncertainty of all things future, so far as this world is concerned. And such warnings are unspeakable mercies, designed by God for the most wise and benevolent purposes.

The season of amended health, and present suspension of painful and distressing symptoms, is precisely that in which your heart should exercise a peculiar jealousy over itself, lest the comparative trifles of this world, and the ensnaring affections of the flesh, should deaden your feelings about the grand question, "What are the evidences of my salvation? What have I done, what must I do to be saved?" Other studies than those directly religious *may*, doubtless, have their due and subordinate place. Other books than the holy Scriptures, and their expositions, may also have their moderated share of our attention; but if any human study, or any human book, have more of our love and attention, than those which directly lead our hearts to God, something must be very wrong. Idols force themselves upon our notice everywhere, and lawful things may become idols by the abuse of them, and the suffering them to usurp the *first* place in the heart's affections. Never be contented with slight and general hopes of all being right within, but seek and strive after clear and particular evidences that you "know whom you have trusted," for time and eternity. I earnestly entreat you to examine yourself daily on scriptural principles, that you may the more ardently throw yourself on the mercy of a covenant God for the forgiveness of your sins, the renovation of your heart, and the guidance of your judgment. Never be satisfied with an avowedly imperfect Christianity. A *half* Christian is *no* Christian, nor is he accepted of God. Christ is a whole, perfect, and finished Saviour; and whosoever is a partaker of Christ, is a partaker of *all* that he is, all that he has done, and all that he will do, for the complete salvation of all his chosen. Decency formality, and cold ceremonial worship, are poor and inefficacious substitutes for heart-service, holy affections, trust in a Saviour, and love to God. Not unfrequent are the times, and your dear mother often experiences them also, when the immensity of that question, "Am I his, or am I not?" overwhelms me; and I should sink in despondency, if the pure, undeserved, and inexpressible mercy of God, did not direct my soul to the Redeemer's blood, which, when believed in, and applied to the guilty and trembling conscience, cleanseth from all sin, and opens the door to hope and consolation. May my beloved child flee to the same fountain with genuine humiliation, and find the like deliverance: and may his anxious parents be made so far partakers of his thoughts, as to feel strong in the Lord on *his* account. My mind was much affected when I first received you at the table of the Lord, and my heart went out in lively prayer, that you might also be received of God—owned, honored, and accepted, as a child of heaven. Live, speak, and act as a consistent communicant of the church; the vows of the Lord are upon you; but if all be right, you will find that his yoke is easy, and his burden light. I wish to look upon you, not only as my child by nature, but as my spiritual child, and therefore, without a paradox, my spiritual *brother*. Sweet associations of relationship are formed in the family of God and the household of faith. Many tender and affectionate prayers have been daily offered up for you amongst the poor people of Turvey, as I have several testimonies to prove. We shall soon return to them again, God willing; and may those prayers, united to my own, be fully answered in the gracious state of your soul, as well as in the comfort of your bodily health. But we must, as to the latter, await the Lord's will. He doeth, and will do all things well. Meditate on these things, and may you and I mutually reap the benefit of such exercises of your heart. As you read this letter, cherish a tender as well as a dutiful sentiment towards him who penned it, and accept it as one more token of that deep-seated love which I bear towards you, and which must increasingly subsist, while *I* remain a father, and *you* a son.

I yesterday enjoyed the high mental luxury of walking in the broad aisle of York Minster, quite alone, during the morning service. As often before, such sights and such sounds compelled me to weep; and as I was solitary, nothing interrupted the flow of my heart. I recollected being there once with you, and I have not forgotten how much, if I mistake not, your infant heart was also affected at that time. Whether we shall ever again meet together, in that magnificent and astonishing fabric, I know not; but oh! may God grant that we finally meet in the "house not made with hands, eternal in the heavens."[1]

*To his daughter Fanny.*

Turvey, December, 1824

I think, dearest Fanny, that the plan which I suggested will be best for your return home; give me a letter to precede you. "Hic sumus," (here we are) quiet, comfortable, and uniform in our daily course,

---

1  2 Corinthians 5:1.

without many striking events to diversify it by day or by night, unless it be that the younger bairns are rather noisy by day, and the cats in the garden outrageously so by night. Mamma is detained at Bath, by the lingering and precarious state of Mrs. C——. Willy is not materially different. My dear, much-loved boy. No one will ever know what I have inwardly undergone on his account since May last. I have no reason to doubt that his mind is in a good state, but I think its exercises are somewhat too dependent on the fluctuations of his body. I entreat you, when restored to his companionship, to second every wish of my heart in promoting serious, devotional, and determinate piety and occupation of heart. I sometimes fear that his mind is too playful, too comparatively careless, in the midst of carefulness. He is an invalid of too precarious a class to trifle, or to be trifled with. Watch over his besetting-infirmities, and aim, without appearing to intend it, to correct them.

Many persons, God be praised, appear at this time to be under serious impressions, and the Lord's work in this parish is evidently progressing. I earnestly wish to see it so under my own roof, as well as in my neighbors' cottages. Yes, my Fanny, my own loved child, I wish to witness more positive, decided, unequivocal demonstrations of it in your own heart. Beware of substituting mere sentimentalism for vital experience; and any, however subtle, species of idolatry for the simple, sincere, unsophisticated love of Jesus—Jesus, the sinner's refuge—Jesus, the sinner's friend—Jesus, the sinner's companion. Beware of the fascinating but dangerous tribe of poets, fictionists, story-tellers, and dramatists, whose writings steal away the heart from God, secretly poison the spring of devotion, create false standards of judgment, and rob God of his honor. Never let the ignis fatuus[1] of genius beguile you into the swamps and puddles of immorality, much less of infidelity: the heart is deceitful above all things, and desperately wicked; who can know it? Ten thousand thieves and robbers within are continually purloining God of our best affections; they assume imposing attitudes, array themselves

1 Ignis Fatuus—A misleading influence; a decoy. (1913 Wester's Dictionary)

in false attire, speak flattering words, "prophesy smooth things," delude the imagination, and darken the soul. Watch and pray, that ye enter not into temptation. Always keep a searching experimental book in private reading, to accompany the study and daily reading of the word of God. Beware of trifling and mere gossiping conversation, even with religious friends; the aforenamed thieves and robbers are never more active than under the plausible guise of unprofitable intercourse with those whom on good grounds we esteem.

"The time is short," should be written on every one and every thing we see. Dear Charlotte Buchanan is now gone to the rest that remaineth for the people of God. Do you not now feel, that had you anticipated so speedy a bereavement, many a thought would have been cherished, many a word uttered, many a conversation held, more congenial with the idea of her early flight from time to eternity, from the visible to the invisible world? But you know not who may go next. If, then, where health may still bloom on the cheek, so much consideration is due; how much more so, when sickness and anticipated decay warn us, that those we love may not long be with us. I deeply feel that our general standard of social and domestic religion is too low. It does not sufficiently partake of the more simple and pure vitality of the poor man's piety. The cottage outstrips the drawing-room, in the genuine characteristics of the gospel efficacy.

. . . There is not only to be found in the religious world, a solid, substantial, consistent, and devoted character, but there is also what may be termed a pretty, genteel sort of evangelism, which too well combines with the luxurious ease and partial acquiescence of the world and the flesh, not to say the devil also. But such evangelism will not prepare the soul for sickness, death, and eternity; or will, at best, leave it a prey to the most fearful doubts, or, still more to be feared, the delusions of false peace. The way that leads to eternal life is much more narrow than many of our modern professors are aware of; the gate is too strait to allow all their trifling, and self-will, and fastidiousness, and carnal-mindedness to press through it. The Gospel is a system of self-denial; its dictates teach us to strip ourselves, that we may clothe others; they leave us hungry, that we may have wherewith to feed others; and send us barefooted among the thorns of the world, rather than silver-shod, with mincing steps, to walk at our ease amongst its snares. When our Lord was asked, "Are there few that shall be saved?" he answered neither yes nor no, but said, "*Strive* to enter in at the strait gate";[1] and this word "strive" might be translated "agonize." Beware of belonging to that class which Mrs. H. ingeniously calls "the borderers." Choose whom you will serve, and take care not to prefer Baal. Ask yourself every night, What portion of the past day have I given to God, to Christ, to devotion, to improvement, to benevolent exertion, to effectual growth in grace? Weep for the deficiencies you therein discover, and pray for pardon and brighter progress. We intend next Thursday to give a little feast to a great company of the poor children of Turvey. Dear Willy will not be able this year to explain the magic lantern, and talk to them about "Lions and Whittingtons," so we must try to be optical without. H—— will act behind the scenes, but make no speeches.

. . . I hope to hear a better account of Mrs. W——, to whom present my very affectionate regards. From my heart I wish you a merry Christmas, and a happy New-year when it comes. St. James explains "merry," James 5:13;[2] so does our Lord, Luke 15:24.[3] May such merry-makings be ours. Our love to all. Tell Mr. M. to write to Wilberforce. I want correspondents who will do him good, and not trifle. I am to preach two missionary sermons at Cambridge on the thirteenth. Farewell, my beloved Fanny; come quickly here, and be assured how truly I am,

Your faithful loving father,

LEGH RICHMOND

---

1 Luke 13:23, 24.

2 James 5:13—Is any among you afflicted? let him pray. Is any merry? let him sing psalms.

3 Luke 15:24—For this my son was dead, and is alive again; he was lost, and is found. And they began to be merry.

*To the same.*

JANUARY 6, 1825

My DEAR FANNY—Your communication is just such as I wish you often and again to repeat. Let your heart be confidential, and you will ever find mine responsive to it. . . . May no trifles ever wean your affections from the unspeakably important subjects of eternity. Idols are bewitching, dangerous things, and steal away the heart from God. The most lawful things may become idols, by fixing an unlawful degree of affection upon them. One reason of the difficulties with which you meet on the subject of prayer may be, the not sufficiently looking by faith unto Christ. Essential as prayer is, both as a privilege, an evidence, an instrument of good, and a source of every blessing; yet it is only the intercessory prayer of Christ, that can render our prayers acceptable and efficacious, and it is only by lively faith in the great Intercessor, that we can obtain a heart to pray. Thus faith and prayer act in a kind of circle in our minds, and each produces, (experimentally) and is produced, by the aid of the other. I am glad you like Mr. Bickersteth's little book on prayer; all his publications are good. There are many books, as well as general conversations *about* religious matters, which, after all, do not bring home true religion to the heart. Religious gossiping is a deceitful thing, and deceives many. How many professors of religion will utter twenty flippant remarks, pro or con, upon a preacher, where one will lay his remarks to his heart. How many look more to the vessel than the excellency of the treasure contained in it. Some people cannot relish their tea or coffee, unless served in a delicate cup with a pretty pattern and a gilt edge. Let poor dear Charlotte Buchanan's sudden call from time to eternity, warn us how needful it is to "die daily"; not to trifle with our souls, when eternity may be so near; nor to boast of the morrow, when we know not what a day may bring forth. Willy is anxious for your return; he droops at present, and wishes to have his dearest friends near him. . . . I rejoice to find your recent meditations have opened to your conscience besetting infirmities. Press forward, my child, let them not gain an ascendency. Beware of mere sentimentalism, of satire, of fastidiousness towards persons and things. Beware of bigotry and prejudice, of procrastination, of the love of fictions, of dangerous, though fascinating poets, etc. . . . I wish you, my love, to attach yourself to visiting the sick, and conversing usefully with the poor; to the instruction of poor children; to *religious* correspondence and conversation with a *few* sincere friends; and particularly, strive to commence and continue spiritual conversation with our dear Willy.

I lately watched the young moon declining in the western sky—it shone sweetly. Sometimes a cloud shot across the disk—sometimes a floating mist partially obscured it, alternately it was bright again: it sometimes silvered the edge of the very cloud that hid it from sight. At length the lower horn touched the horizon, then the upper horn, and then it wholly disappeared. Venus remained to cheer the gloom. I said to myself, *"There* is the decline of my loved boy, and *there* is the star of hope."

Your affectionate father,

L. RICHMOND

# Chapter 4

LETTER TO HIS SON-IN-LAW, AFTER THE DEATH OF
WILBERFORCE—TO HIS ELDEST DAUGHTER—TO HIS
YOUNGER CHILDREN—TO HIS SON-IN-LAW AND THIRD
DAUGHTER, PREVIOUS TO THEIR MARRIAGE—TO HIS
YOUNGER CHILDREN—TO HIS ELDER DAUGHTERS—TO
HENRY, WHO WAS ABOUT TO ENTER THE UNIVERSITY—
MEDITATION WRITTEN SHORTLY PREVIOUS TO HIS DEATH

*To his Son-in-law, after the death of his beloved Wilberforce.*

TURVEY, JAN. 25, 1825

MY MUCH-LOVED SON—Amidst many arduous struggles between nature and grace, sorrow and joy, anxiety and consolation, I wish to express a few of my feelings towards you. A very few they must be, compared with the volume of emotions which agitate my heart. But, thanks be to God, grace, peace, and mercy have been so abundantly inscribed upon the whole of this affecting transaction, that I ought solely to be occupied in songs of praise to God, for all his goodness to me and mine. The delightful enlargement of heart, the liberty of tongue, the humiliation of soul, the affectionate tenderness, the sweet serenity of mind, the dignity of sentiment, the laboriously acquired intimacy with the Scriptures, the earnestness to speak, to exhort, and comfort each and every individual, the devotional spirit, the clearness of doctrinal views, and their blessed application in imparting solid peace and comfort, in the prospect of dying, all of which illustrated and adorned his latter end, were beyond my most sanguine expectation: it was, and shall be, matter for joy and gratitude.

We have now found letters, some of them near four years old, and others written while he was in Scotland, beautifully descriptive of his state of mind; while the conversations—close, deep, and searching—which I enjoyed with him during the last fortnight, produced the most convincing demonstrations that he had been ripening for glory, beyond our thoughts and imaginations. For a season, he was reserved towards me relative to personal feelings; but at length, of his own accord, he broke out like the sun from behind a cloud, and light diffused itself over the whole moral and spiritual landscape.

It was gratifying to me to find that the humiliation of his spirit was precisely such as I particularly wished to see it. For four or five days previous to the arrival of my wife and Fanny, God so mercifully ordered it, that he said every thing to me, and I to him, which I could possibly have wished. Our whole souls, on almost every topic of feeling, opinion, confidence, faithful dealing, and unreserved affection, were mutually opened. Oh, they were sweet days. The pressure of weakness, disease, and pain, often afterwards interrupted our lengthened communications; but sweeter and brighter still were the intervals of ease and short conversation. Many witnessed his lovely testimonies, and none can ever forget them.

Two hours and a half before his death, he went to bed, and laid his head upon the pillow. I said to him, "So he giveth his beloved rest." He replied, "Yes; and sweet indeed is the rest which Christ gives." He never awoke from this sleep; but when we dreaded, from past examples, a painful waking, he imperceptibly went off, in perfect peace, without a sigh, or groan, or struggle, or even opening of the eye. I did not suppose it possible for any death to be such as this. Peace, rest, gentleness, faith, hope, and love, all seemed to be the characteristics of his mind and of his dissolution. Oh, what love, what mercy, what grace.

One of the most remarkable circumstances attending him was, his secret and deep exercise of heart and study of the Scriptures, beyond my own supposition, owing to his reserve and silence. I saw much that I loved and admired, but I was not aware of the half. Our feelings are much tried in proportion to the endearing nature of our past and recent intercourse. But, as he often said, "I know whom I have trusted," and this relieves and consoles me. He was *deeply* impressed with the idea that his removal was designed for the spiritual good of others. I think it is manifest already, in more instances than one.

The whole village has been much in prayer and weeping, for some weeks past, and the tenderest affections have prevailed throughout: it is a season of much love.

On Sunday, Mr. Ayre will preach a funeral sermon for our dear boy; and a beautiful hymn of Bishop Heber will be sung by the congregation.

Give my tenderest love to dear Mary. Comfort her heart; and may the peace of God, which passeth all understanding, keep hers and your heart.

TO THE REV. JAMES MARSHALL
*To his eldest daughter, Mrs. Marshall.*

TURVEY, FEB. 6, 1825

MY EVER-DEAR CHILD— . . . And now to the subject which occupies by far the greater part of my thoughts, by day and by night. I should find it no easy task to describe the state of my feelings. No previous event of my life, with the exception of what passed during your beloved mother's dangerous illness, near ten years since, ever exercised my heart like this. And as that illness terminated favorably, the circumstances no longer assimilate. Dear, blessed boy, I watched over and cherished his infancy, childhood, and youth, in sickness and in health, for eighteen years, with no common measure of parental feeling. I delighted in his superior mind; endeavored to check its errors, and to cherish its virtues; and too fondly hoped that he might have been spared as an ornament to the sanctuary. From the beginning of last summer I went on pilgrimage with him, both for his soul and body's sake. God alone knows what I endured, in the inmost thoughts of my heart. But the Lord was ordering all things well, beyond what I conceived. The most valuable intercourse which I enjoyed with him during our Scotch residence, was in those hours after breakfast, when, as you may remember, I used to read, talk, and pray with him, previous to his receiving the sacrament at Greenock, I then saw many lovely testimonies of his state of mind. After his return home, he was more reserved as to the personal question, although ever ready to converse on the general subjects of religion, and that with much clearness and precision. But at length the sweet sunshine broke from the cloud, and filled the horizon most beautifully. We poured out our whole hearts to each other, and mutually blessed God for the liberty of feeling and language which we obtained. I felt much when he had just departed, but I think I feel more now. A thousand spiritual questions press upon my conscience and consideration. Regrets, convictions, meltings, hopes, fears, doubts, resolutions, anxieties, joys, retrospections, anticipations, all mingle, all exercise, all agitate my heart. It was his declared and solemn impression, that his death was to be as life to others. Thank God, I see it so, both in the house and the parish—an important work is going on in both, beyond former precedent. I have not seen the like before, to the same extent. Blessed be God!

Dear Willy told me, on the Monday evening before he died, that Mr. M——'s affectionate attentions to him had never been exceeded by those of a real brother; and that he should love him dearly as long as he lived, and "much longer," he said, "if such consciousness shall be permitted. And dear Mary," he added, "how kind she was to us all, last summer. I shall not see her again on earth, but I trust we shall meet hereafter." Our last Lord's supper was a very affecting and trying one: the family kneeled around the grave, to which we had recently committed the mortal remains of one so dear. I stood upon the very spot; and dear Henry, for the first time, came weeping, trembling, and rejoicing, to supply his departed brother's place. I could hardly have conceived that after so long meditating upon the probable removal of my child from this mortal scene, I should have had such exquisitely trying emotions to undergo. How little we know ourselves until our principles and feelings are put to the proof.

*To his fourth Son.*

MY DEAR L——, I leave these few lines with you, in the hope that you will reply to them while I am in Cambridge. You must write, therefore, not later than by Tuesday's post. I do from my heart desire to know whether you do, or do not, feel an anxiety about your soul's salvation. Has the affecting thought, "I must live for ever in heaven or hell," suitably impressed your mind? This black border may remind you of your dear departed brother; but does his memory live in your heart for good? It is time you seriously reflected on eternity, and the value of your soul. You are a sinner; and without a gracious Saviour you must perish. Do you pray in Christ's name, and that earnestly, for the pardon of your sins? May I hope that you are a penitent? Do you think of Willy's last words to you, and of all that he so earnestly recommended to your serious attention? Have you written down his dying words, as I desired you? Be not afraid to open your mind to me. Let us have an unreserved intercourse with each other. Put away childish things; imitate your brother's love of learning, but especially his love of the Bible, and his constancy in the exercises of devotion. Oh, comfort your father's heart, by truly turning to God, and seeking his salvation; and may God bless you for ever and ever, which is the fervent prayer of your affectionate parent,

L. R.

*To his fourth Daughter.*

MY DEAR CHILD—I am pleased, much pleased with your letter, the more so as it contains some expressions which inspire a hope that you are beginning to think and feel seriously about your soul's salvation. While I cannot but be most tenderly affected by the loss of my two elder sons, endeared to me by a thousand recollections, I become the more anxious for the welfare of those children whom God spares to me. For the last year I have gone through great trials, and my health has suffered more than any are aware of; but in the midst of all my sorrows, the inexpressible goodness of God has been most manifest, and I trust my afflictions have been blest to many. Many a rose has sprung up around the cold grave of dear Willy, and they still blossom, and I trust, will continue to blossom, till they be transplanted from the spiritual garden of Turvey, to the paradise of God. But can I be otherwise than anxious that my dear K—— should add a flower to my domestic and parochial shrubbery. Are you to reach your sixteenth year, and not prove yourself a partaker of the grace of God? I trust not; but religion is not a matter of mere circumstantials, or of morals. It is the spiritual application of divine truth to the heart, producing that devotedness to God which distinguishes the true from the nominal Christian. But when, how, and where does this begin? Not until you have deep, humbling, sincere, and anxious thoughts about yourself, and the favor of God; not until, by a kind of holy violence, you feel constrained to flee to Christ, as the only refuge from the wrath to come; not until prayer becomes importunate, and the study of God's word a delight; not until every other consideration yields to that infinitely important inquiry, "What must I do to be saved?" not until the light, trifling, and thoughtless child of man be converted, through grace, to the serious, conscientious, and believing state of the real child of God. Is this the case with you? I speak as a Christian father, and minister. What are your views of these important subjects? I wish my child to be deeply earnest: life flies apace, the period of the tomb advances. I have four children in eternity; it is true, that eight more still continue with me on earth, but O how long will they be here? Which of them may next be taken from me? I think on these things with deep solemnity. You tremble at the thought of a school-examination; but what is this to the examination before the judgment-seat of God. Go, then, as a sinner to Christ. He sends none empty away. In him, and him alone, there is a rich provision for all who come to him. But let this coming mean a surrender of all you are, and all you have, to the Lord of grace and glory. Be contented with nothing short of reality in religion.

Whence came I? memory cannot say;
   What am I? knowledge will not show;
Bound whither? ah, away—away—
   Far as eternity can go;
Thy love to win, thy wrath to flee,
Oh God, thyself my helper be.

Farewell, my dear child, and believe me

Your truly loving father,

L. R.

*To his daughter Fanny and his son Henry.*

LONDON, JUNE, 1825

DEAR FANNY AND DEAR HENRY—Between the morning and evening services of this day, I have a leisure hour, in which I feel as if I should like to sit down and talk with you two. I miss our early morning exercises much, and this for the present must be the substitute on my part. I have nothing very particular to recount, only that I have been to a few places where I was last summer with my beloved Wilberforce, and I have indulged the silent tear as I retraced incidents never again to recur. At some places, where my friends remember his visits and conversations, I am asked "how he is," with interest in their manner, and have to tell how he has taken his flight to another and a better world; and it affects me greatly so to do. I know not how it is with me, in regard to that dear boy's loss, but I talk less and think more than ever about him. The fortnight preceding, and the one succeeding his death, are indelibly graven on my heart's recollections, and sometimes overpower me in a way of which none of you have any real idea. Sometimes my mind is strengthened, but at others weakened by these reflections. I am sometimes comforted, at others terrified by these exercises of the mind. With what liveliness do the scenes of our northern tour press upon my mind: the lovely Isle of Bute with all its magnificent scenery; the incomparable beauties of Loch-Lomond, and Loch-Long, with their hospitable friendships; the wild loveliness of Inverary, and Loch-Awe; the fine views on the Firth of Clyde, with the moral and intellectual characteristics of many a kind friend; the steam-boats, the carts, the cars, the mountains, all associate with *him*, and are endeared to me beyond expression. I linger over all the spots we visited together, from Loch-Awe to Glasgow, Carlisle, Keswick, Woodhouse, Matlock, etc., to Turvey. I love to think of our private reading in my little bedroom at Rothsay, his first communion at Greenock, and then to connect all with his closing days. It is my weakness, my fault, my misfortune, that I cannot express more of my mind and feelings to you both. Dear, dear Henry, you are now become the prop and stay of my declining years; think much of the station in which God has placed you. My first-born is a distant wanderer, and God knows when or whether I shall see him again on earth. My second boy is taken from me; you are my third, but now my first. Be such to your two brothers, particularly to L———; he needs your constant superintending care; watch over him, do not leave him to seek unprofitable associates; cherish the little germ of hope which God has planted in my bosom concerning him; let your example influence, and your kind attentions encourage him in every good way; and think much of your own soul. Beware of declensions: remember the last words of dear Wilberforce; live up to his advice. How my heart yearns over you, and all your prospects. What are you? What are you to be, my loved child? Write to me freely.

And my Fanny also: are you as much alive to spiritual things, as when you hastened to the dying bed of dear Willy; as when you wept over his coffin? My child, dread *all* decays, and may the flame of spiritual piety never grow-dim amidst the mists of unworthier speculations. Visit the cottages; forsake not the poor, for your father's sake.

I have been this morning where you might least have expected to find me; but I went not from curiosity, but from a conscientious wish to know and judge for myself; namely, to the Roman Catholic chapel in Moorfields, to hear high mass. I was astonished at the decorations, the gorgeous dresses of the bishop and priests, charmed with the exquisite beauty of the music, disgusted at the ceremonial mummery of the service, and unconvinced by the bishop's eloquent sermon in defense of transubstantiation. It was all illusion, delusion, and collusion. The service lasted near four hours. I bless God more than ever for true Protestantism. I shall hear the Messiah performed tomorrow. Such music I love, it lifts my soul to heaven. I am sick and disgusted with common light modern songs; they are unfit for Christians. Oh, what music is my Willy enjoying in heaven. Shall we all enjoy it with him? The question often sinks me in the dust. My dear, my most dear children, press forward to the prize of the mark of our high calling in Christ Jesus. There is an immense gulf to be passed. Who is sufficient for these things?

Say truly kind and pastoral things for me to my dear people at Turvey. Truly I have them in my heart. My children all, I kiss you from a distance; believe how much and how tenderly I love you.

*     *     *     *     *

P. S.—MONDAY—I am just returned from hearing the Messiah. In the two grand choruses, I thought I could hear my Willy's voice, and it quite overcame me. Past, present, and future, mingled in strange and affecting combination. These feelings are sometimes too much for your poor father.

The following letters are addressed to his son-in-law and third daughter, previous to their marriage.

MY DEAR FRIEND—On consulting Mrs. R. and our dear H———, they both agree that the beginning of July is the earliest period at which the object in view can be accomplished. So, leaving it in their hands, I simply put my seal of approbation and consent to their decision; and I do so with a heart full of love and esteem for you both. May God bless your prospects, and your souls in them. I love all my children too well not to say, that in committing Henrietta into your hands, I give you one of my cherished treasures, and sources of domestic endearment. I feel parting with my daughter the more, from the removal of my loved, my much-loved Wilberforce. His death, with all its affecting associations, has had a peculiar, I trust a very useful effect upon all my feelings, sentiments, ministrations, prospects, and thoughts, for time and eternity. The subject is wound up with my heart's experience, in a way I can never describe. I pray God to overrule it for the present and eternal good of myself and my dear family. Yours, very truly and affectionately,

L. R.

TURVEY, JULY 6, 1825

My dear Henrietta—Take, my beloved child, a father's blessing, prayers, best wishes, and approval of your affectionate project. I hope the matter is of God, or I could not say what I have done. The apostolical rule is, to "marry only in the Lord"; and every Christian should be guided by it. Earthly affection, however powerful, is not of itself a warrant for the nuptial union. Where passion drives the steeds by which the vehicle of our plans and endeavors is carried forward, we may expect, sooner or later, an overturn. But when the heavenly Spirit of truth and peace guides and governs our machinery of conduct, all is right and safe. Now I am full of hope, from Mr. Ayre's and your letters, that this is the case. Real Christianity as a foundation, with personal esteem and affection, united to congeniality of feelings on all important subjects, as a superstructure, will ever make the marriage union a source of happiness for both worlds.

I am disposed to concur with you in thinking that my esteemed friend's principles, acquirements, talents, and steadiness of character, are good pledges of his success in life; and as Providence, not design, first brought you together, and seems to have guided you both, I feel myself justified in joining my consent and sanction to the future realizing of those views which form the subject of his and your letters to me. May constancy, faithfulness, and reciprocal love, characterize your attachment, and adorn your conduct. Let prudence, propriety, and consideration regulate all your behavior, during the interval which must naturally elapse before all is concluded. Keep in mind the dignity as well as the kindliness of the Christian lover; courtship and marriage are honorable in all, when principle and grace direct our choice. May you prove a blessing to each other, and may the love of God be shed abroad in both your hearts.

MY DEAR FRIEND—Of all human connections and projects, none appears to be of more importance than that of marriage. Whatever is valuable in private life, whatever is prosperous in public life, whatever is scriptural in spiritual life, and whatever is momentous in eternal life, has a deep foundation laid, in the economy of Providence and grace, in marriage. It should be built upon the purest principles of faith, hope, and love. It unites two souls for time and eternity. It educates souls for the church of God. It forms, or reforms, or deforms character. It blesses or it curses. It makes happy or miserable. It brings every precept of religion into active exercise. Therefore, when rightly undertaken, "marriage is honorable in all." You, my friend, I am persuaded, are convinced of these truths, and I doubt not wish to prove it in the present instance.

I trust the providence of God is in the matter, and that you and my dear child will be guided for the best in every thing connected with the subject. My prayer is, that grace may reign throughout, and that you may prove helpmates to each other in your pilgrimage through this to a better world.

My heart often sinks within me, when I see how little solid, sterling, *vital piety* manifests itself, even amongst many creditable Christians. I the more earnestly pray for myself, and for all belonging to me, that we may walk circumspectly, redeeming the time amidst evil days. How much more of the Spirit's influence do we all need. When I look back upon a half century of rational existence, I blush, and take shame to myself. How much *done* which I might wish *undone;* and *not done,* that ought to have been *done.*

The publican's prayer is mine, and will alone suit me, even to my dying hour.

Farewell, for a short interval, and believe me

Affectionately yours,

Legh Richmond

He also presented his daughter with a paper entitled, "Marriage admonitions to Henrietta, from her affectionate father,

"L. R."

My much-loved Daughter—When your sister Mary left her paternal roof, I gave her a paper of admonitions, which I requested her sometimes to read for her own and for her father's sake. I do the same for you, in the form of a friendly string of maxims, to regulate your conduct in your new and very responsible situation.

1. Aim at keeping a devoted heart for God in the least and most common transactions of every hour, as well as in those events which may seem to call the loudest for manifestations of religious conscience and principle.

2. Pray regularly and frequently, not seldom and occasionally, for grace to live and die by.

3. Remember the principles and professions of your father's house, and everywhere endeavor to preserve its character, by consistency in conduct, conversation, and temper.

4. Form no hasty intimacies, and none whatever but such as may promote seriousness of heart, tongue, and demeanor.

5. Beware of cheerfulness degenerating into levity, and ignorance of the world into prejudice.

6. Guard against hasty judgments of character, and above all, against hastily uttering sentiments and making remarks to the disparagement of others.

7. Wherever you are, not only remember that God's eye is upon you, but imagine to yourself that your husband and father are also present. It may be a fanciful, but it is a profitable supposition.

8. Keep in constant recollection the wise, prudent, and conscientious example of your dear mother. Be cautious when in religious company, and endeavor to sustain a deportment which may induce the excellent of the earth to desire your society for their own sake as well as yours.

9. Particularly avoid making the errors, failings, faults, or follies of good people, either in private or public matters, the subject of rash and unguarded remarks. Be known for charity, forbearance, and kindness.

10. Keep Christ's golden rule, Luke 6:31,[1] in perpetual remembrance; it is the panacea for most of the evils of life, so far as they are connected with social intercourse.

11. Entertain no prejudices against nations, churches, sects, or parties; they are the bane of truth, chanty, and comfort, and are directly opposed to the letter and spirit of Christianity. You may and ought to have a conscientious, well-founded preference, but not one half-formed, ill-formed prejudice against any one.

12. Be conscientious towards all, friendly with few, intimate with fewer still, strictly confidential with fewest of all.

13. From the hour you marry, you assume the character of a matron; be not a childish, girlish wife; the vows of God are upon you, sustain their gravity and prudence in all things.

14. If circumstances and friendly connections lead you into the superintendence of charitable institutions, enter upon your office with prayer and consideration, and persevere in the discharge of its duties with patience and well-guided zeal.

15. Let no natural vivacity of temper, no occasionally indulged sallies of humor and jocularity throw a shade over the exercise of solid principle. Little foolish things give a color to character, and are more easily caught at than grave and good sentiments.

16. All eyes are sure to be fixed on a young wife; beware of, while you conform to, that sort of bridal publicity which is necessarily

---

1 Luke 6:31—And as ye would that men should do to you, do ye also to them likewise.

connected with every circle of residents and acquaintance.

17. Choose female intimacies with circumspection: many civil, hospitable, agreeable persons, are far from being improving companions; we may owe and pay them the debt of civility, kindness, and gratitude, and yet not be obliged to give them too much of our time and affection. Two or three truly Christian women form a circle sufficiently large for profitable friendship.

18. In every, however small a circle of acquaintance, you will find more or less of party-spirit, prejudice, and too great freedom of remark on persons and circumstances connected with them: beware of making one of these. Be slow to judge, rather than swift to speak; the best Christians often fail here.

19. You are much given to laughter, my dear child, and many a hearty laugh I have enjoyed with you, and I would not turn your laughter into sorrow, but this propensity may prove a snare to you. Watch and be jealous of it; banish what looks like giggling, lightness, and folly, and cultivate a chastened cheerfulness and simplicity of manner in all companies.

20. Never forget that you are entering an entire circle of strangers, and that a very few weeks or months will establish your character amongst them.

Once more, I say, think of your father's house and reputation. When I look upon myself and all that belongs to me, I feel ashamed of my own feeble, faint attempts to serve God and adorn his gospel; yet the Christian world has attached to them, however undeservedly, a value, and by the name and character of their father will my children be tried and appreciated.

21. Keep indelibly engraven on your heart the affecting scenes of last January. A dying brother's faithful admonitions—his last words, his last looks of mortal affection. Our household never witnessed the like, was never so tried. The memorials dwell on my heart with increasing poignancy. I say less, but I feel more; there is a solemn, silent, softening, and subduing influence, which often overwhelms me. May you retain a vivid recollection, with a perpetuated blessing,

of that day when our Wilberforce fled from earth to heaven.

22. Be especially attentive to the opinion which your demeanor may inspire amongst your husband's relations. No doubt he has praised you before them; endeavor to prove in all points that he has done you no more than justice: much family peace and love depends upon this.

23. There are many excellent hints in the book entitled, "A Whisper to a New-married Pair." I recommend them to your perusal. And there are many more excellent hints to wives and women in the Bible, from Solomon, Paul, and Peter; study them well.

24. When you think of your father, bear with his infirmities, pardon his faults, but remember his principles and instructions, so far as they have been agreeable to the will of God.

25. Be not contented with anything short of deep, devoted, diligent, decided seriousness. Make not the too numerous half-hearted and decent, but dubious Christians, your patterns for imitation. Set your mark and standard very high, and aim deliberately to regulate your conduct by it.

26. If you and your husband happen to differ in opinion or feeling in any point, remember whom you have promised to love, honor, and obey, and this will settle all things.

27. Of your husband's warm affections towards you, I entertain no doubt; strive to preserve them by daily elevation of character, not so much by fondness as by prudence and dignity. Study his character, he will study yours. May you both learn to raise a fabric of connubial happiness by mutual wisdom and love.

28. I trust you are taught in the school of Christ; rely not, however, on the past privileges of education, but seek present evidences, such as will comfort you under sudden alarms and distresses, should they occur. Try to get acquainted with yourself by a review of your whole life, and often carry to the Lord in prayer and confidence, the results of examination into your heart and conduct.

29. Observe great simplicity and plainness in dress. A clergyman's wife should be a pattern to others in these respects; there

is a just complaint made of many females who profess to be religious, that they are far too showy and gay in their outward apparel; remember the apostle's injunction—1 Peter 3:1–6.

30. Never, think yourself too old to learn; the most valuable period of education is perhaps from twenty to forty years of age. The matured mind is *fittest to become the little child.*

31. You are bidding farewell to your father's house, the home of your infancy, childhood, and youth; yet the remembrance of the principles in which you have been educated should follow you through life, wherever divine Providence may see fit to call you. May they be a guide to you at all times, a consolation to you in your final removal from a sinful and changing world.

Christ has been made known to you fully and freely: let Christ be your *all in all*, both now and for ever. Receive my parting advice in love, and be assured, my beloved child, it comes from the affectionate heart of

Your dear father,

L. R.

To C——, ON HER BIRTHDAY—I cannot let a parcel go to Y—— without telling my dear C—— how much her father loves her. This is a day of grateful recollections, and hopeful anticipations. God bless my child. May she grow in grace with increasing years; may she be diligent in her studies, docile in disposition, devotionally fervent in spirit, and unwearied in well-doing.

My anxieties have been great since I saw you. My heart has so clung to my dear boy, that every tender feeling and affection has been exercised in the separation from my beloved Wilberforce; but the loss has not diminished, but increased my love to the endeared children whom God still spares to me. I cannot say one thousandth part of what I would on this subject, but my heart prays that you may all grow in the knowledge of Him with whom *his* soul now lives in blessedness. I hope much good has arisen to your brothers and sisters at home from the sanctified effect of this heavy trial.

May my C—— feel it likewise, and so experience the power of real religion in her heart, that it may appear in her life and conversation. I am *very* anxious on this subject. A great work of gracious awakening has taken place in the village, in connection Wilberforce's happy end. Many careless souls are surprisingly changed. This is a mercy, an unspeakable mercy to me as their minister. Oh, I want *all* my children to share abundantly in these dews of heavenly grace. I earnestly covet for them these best gifts. Others will have told you by this parcel how much *they* love you. This letter can but very feebly say how dear you are in the love of a Saviour.

From your affectionate father,

L. R.

*A birthday letter to his fourth Son.*

MY MUCH-LOVED BOY—You expressed some disappointment at dinner, because you had not received your dear mamma's promised letter on your birthday. What has been the cause of the failure I know not, but I will try to compensate for the disappointment by giving you a few lines. The return of a birthday, when rightly viewed, is a subject for very serious meditation: I wish it may prove so to you. We have seen, in the death of your dear brother, how little health and strength are to be trusted. Childhood and youth, and time, are swiftly passing onward, and our journey through this vale of tears, whether longer or shorter, will soon be over. Can you too early learn the value and importance of time? Will you not hear the counsel of a father, and meditate on those things which belong to your everlasting peace? You have an immortal soul, to be lost or saved for ever. You have an understanding, to distinguish between good and evil. You are therefore a responsible being, who must render an account of the deeds done in the body, whether they be good or whether they be evil. Childhood is the period when the character and habits of the future man are formed. Trifle not, therefore, with your childish days. Set a firm and valuable example to your younger brother: he will more or less imitate your ways and dispositions, be they better or worse. Remember, the eye of God is upon you in every place. Be where you will, do what you will, you may always say with Hagar in the wilderness, "Thou God seest me."[1] I have of late known but little, too little of your state of mind and your views of things, temporal and spiritual. I have had occasional uneasiness on this subject. You ought ever to be putting forth the energies of your mind in every proper and possible way. It is time that your attention should be drawn to your future station in life, whatever Providence may design it to be. Every day and every hour should bear witness to some progress and improvement in useful learning, and above all, in that knowledge which maketh wise unto salvation! You have on all subjects much to learn, and it will not be acquired without much labor, and firm determination of mind and talent to the acquirement. What may be the inclination of your own mind as to business, profession, or occupation, I know not; but I wish you most seriously to take this subject into deliberate consideration, and let me in due time know the result, that I may give you counsel and advice. In the mean time, a thirst for useful knowledge, and a laborious attention to its attainment, will best evidence your fitness for that state of life into which it may please God to call you. But you can do nothing well without faith and prayer; without much anxious reading of the Holy Scriptures. This reminds me of your dear brother Wilberforce. He left upon record amongst you all, *his* testimony to the value and necessity of reading the word of God; and it is my heart's prayer and desire that all my loved children may follow his example and his dying exhortations. The season of the year is fast advancing which brings all the affections and solemnities of his latter end to view. Every day of the approaching fortnight brings to remembrance the various events of his last days. They are all indelibly fastened on my heart's memory; they live, glow, and burn there with a vividness of impression, of which none can be aware, and form a daily part of my very self. But I refer to them now for my dear Legh's sake. I have lost my two eldest boys,

1 Genesis 16:13.

and am deeply solicitous that those who remain to me should be devoted to God; and, if spared, become the props and solace of my advancing years. It is indeed time, my Legh, that you should feel the importance of such considerations. You were named Serle after one of the most holy and excellent men with whom I was ever acquainted. Mere Christian names can confer no grace; but I may be permitted to wish, and hope, and pray, that you may, by divine grace, resemble him, and follow him as he followed Christ. "The Christian Remembrancer," "The Horæ Solitariæ," "The Christian Parent," and many other admirable books, bear testimony to his piety and talents. "He being dead, yet speaketh." And now, my child, may every blessing attend you, for this world and the next, for time and for eternity. May the return of this birthday remind you of many an important duty and principle. Look into the real state of your heart, and never be afraid or ashamed to make me acquainted with it. "The end of all things is at hand; be ye therefore sober, and watch unto prayer."[1] The heart that now loves and watches over you on earth, may ere long, and must, in time, become cold in the grave; but seek Him who never dieth, and *his* love which never decayeth, and all shall be well with you here and hereafter. So counsels and prays

Your affectionate father,

LEGH RICHMOND

*To his daughter Fanny.*

I grant, dearest Fanny, you may charge me with the fault of which you have often been culpable; I have no very good reason to assign for delay, and therefore will rather take my share of blame, than furnish you with a bad argument, or a bad example, in the duty of letter-writing. . . . I rejoice in your account of Turvey, a spot that is always in my mind's eye, when not in my sight. Dear loved parochial and domestic village. Thou art endeared to me by a thousand considerations, both as it respects the living and the dead.

---

1  1 Peter 4:7.

"When I forget thee, let my right hand forget her cunning."[1] No succession of time or circumstances has weaned, or ever can wean my heart from the chancel vault. There is a young triumvirate increasingly endeared to me, one in heaven and two on earth, and their names shall be recorded together—Wilberforce, Henry, and C——. Dear boys, born in the same village, companions in the same school, partners in the same recreations, partakers of the same eucharistic table, friends in every social pursuit, and, dare I say, heirs of the same glory? United by the ties of the same grace on earth, may they share the same felicity in heaven. I am glad that your meditations have been, of late, deep and important. Pray that they may continue so. Life is short, eternity is at hand; banish all needless reserve, banish levity, banish dulness; be much with Christ in prayer, and I had well-nigh added, much with your father in his study. Cultivate an interior acquaintance with Henry, and do all you can with L—— and T——. There is something wanting amongst us, whether in family duet or chorus, as to really improving and spiritual conversation; too much worldly bustle, too much regard to passing events, too much consequent alienation from the one, the only thing needful. Without inquiring who is the most in fault, let each of us strive to resist the evil and cleave to the good. . . . When I think of my boys and C——, I bless God for village seclusion, and greatly rejoice that they have been kept at a comparative distance from the evil communications which corrupt good manners. The world, even in its apparently harmless form, is a terrible snare to the young and uninformed mind. . . . I before gave you my opinion on Sunday evening walks; I have often earnestly denounced them to the people, and need not add a word to you on this head. . . . There is a subject which often hangs heavy on my spirits, I mean my poor dear T——'s inclination for a military life. Hating war as I do from my very heart, convinced as I am of the inconsistency of it with real Christianity, and looking on the profession of arms as irreconcilable with the principles of the Gospel, I should mourn greatly if one of

1 Psalm 137:5.

my boys chose so cruel, and generally speaking, so profligate a line of life. I could never consent to it on conscientious grounds, and therefore wish this bias for the profession of arms to be discouraged. I dislike and oppose it with my whole heart. May God, the *God of peace* bless you, my much-loved Fanny: give a Christian message of pastoral love to my dear flock; I often think and pray for them. Love to the boys. You know well how truly and sincerely I am

Your affectionate father,

LEGH RICHMOND

*To his eldest Daughter.*

TURVEY, OCTOBER 25, 1825

MY DEAREST MARY—I have lately been present at an interesting meeting of the Jewish Auxiliary Society, at Bristol. You know my companions in this journey; I feel better for it. My strength and spirits have been greatly affected for a long time—indescribably so; for it often does not much appear to others, at least not in its real extent. Notwithstanding my supposed readiness of speech, and the overflow of tender feelings which plead for utterance, I am often thoughtful, silent, and constrained, when it might be better for me to communicate more of what passes within.

Our visit to Mrs. Hannah More was a high gratification.

We have been kept in long suspense about poor dear Nugent; he was dangerously ill when I last heard of him. I have reason to expect a speedy letter now arriving in England. I have received rumors of his having died in his passage home, and am fully prepared for the worst; but do not notice what I say until you hear again, as it distresses your dear mother greatly. I thank God, I have had many satisfactory testimonies of his state of mind, and feel much comforted on that head. Henry and I were three weeks under the roof of his intimate and very Christian friend, Lieutenant Bailey, R. N., from Gibraltar, now at Cowes; and collected many interesting circumstances relating to him. I desire to bow to the will of God in this dispensation of his providence. I saw one of his most intimate friends last week, who had just come from the East, and had heard a *report* of his decease. I mention these things to you, that with me you may look up to God for a right state of mind, under all the designs and decrees of his will.

I have had the satisfaction of obtaining likenesses, very nicely executed, in the same style with those of your father and mother, (in the drawing-room) of Fanny, Henry, Henrietta, and Legh. I wish for yours and Mr. Marshall's, by the same hand. My feelings are strong on this subject; and the irrecoverable loss of my dear Wilberforce, and probably of Nugent, render them stronger. It is, I had almost said, a blessed art, which can perpetuate to the eye what affectionate memory does to the heart. In the midst of life we are in death, and who can tell what may occur? I honor the art of painting much, for the sake both of the dead and living. I often look around my study, surrounded as I am by the resemblances of many loved and honored ancestors; and their forms on canvas realize not a few grateful recollections of infancy, childhood, and youth. I can sigh, and weep, and smile, too, in the solitude of my chamber, when I am still, and communing with my own heart.

Just as I finish my letter, I cast my eye on Willy's walking-stick. Oh, how these relics strike to my soul's affections. With our two sticks, alas, he and I wandered on the shores of Rothsay and the adjoining walks, and in many another spot; and now they stand, side by side, in the corner of my study. The partnership of the sticks is preserved on earth, but not that of their possessors: we are separated. Yet, oh that we may be reunited. Meditations on this subject often agitate, sometimes console, always solemnize my mind.

Farewell. Love to your fireside.

*To the same.*

TURVEY, AUGUST 3, 1825

MY EVER-DEAR DAUGHTER— . . . The circumstances attendant upon our dear Nugent's end are few and simple. You are aware what a long series of favorable accounts of his general behavior we have had from a variety of quarters. You should know, that from at least five religious friends I have received highly satisfactory testimonies of his religious feelings and principles, although he was modest and reserved in speaking of himself. I had much information while I was visiting his most intimate friend, Mr. Bailey, in the Isle of Wight, (late of Gibraltar) whose little babe was christened Mercy Nugent Richmond. The time of his shipwreck seemed to have been one of special prayer and impression. He lost his all. He however recruited in some degree; and was engaged to be married to an amiable and pious young lady. He took a short voyage, and on his return found that she had died of a fever. His spirits never recovered that shock. He was afterwards appointed commander of a vessel to England. The day before she sailed, he fell out of a gig, was confined to bed, and lost the opportunity. Twice afterwards he was similarly disappointed. At length he sailed in a ship bound for the Mauritius, from whence he intended to have proceeded to England.

Previously to this last voyage, he had an attack of fever, and went through a severe course of medicine. At the beginning of the voyage, meeting with a heavy gale, he had much laborious service. In the course of a very short time he became ill, and was not unfrequently delirious, but still did not excite ideas of immediate danger. One night, he went to bed at twelve o'clock, and the next morning at six, to the grief and surprise of all on board, was found dead in his cabin. The ship proceeded to the Mauritius; and it was not until her return to Calcutta, that our excellent and kind friend, the Rev. Mr. Thomason, received the news, and his packages, papers, etc. He left, out of the scanty stores preserved from the wreck of the Oracabessa, one hundred rupees to general charitable purposes; fifty to the Bible Society; fifty to the Church Missionary Society; fifty to the Society for Promoting Christian Knowledge; and fifty to the Religious Tract Society. A rupee is about 2s. 6d. His affections for his relatives were very strong. His principles of honorable conduct, integrity, pecuniary accuracy, official diligence, kind manners, and moral deportment, were exemplary. He lived in much esteem, and died much beloved. Dear boy; he was snatched from our embraces at the hour of his returning to them. He is buried in the depths of the ocean. But the sea shall give up her dead, and I trust he will then appear a living soul.

The next letter is to his son Henry, who was just about to enter the university, with a view to the ministry.

CROMER, SEPTEMBER 1, 1826

MY VERY DEAR SON—The time for your destination is not far off, and the word of counsel becomes the more appropriate and needful. From the day wherein you first communicated to me your thoughts and wishes about entering into the sacred ministry, my eye, my heart, my head, my conscience, my tenderest affections, have been steadily fixed upon you, and your future prospects. Until that period, and while your dear brother's health permitted the hope of his becoming a minister, I had other thoughts and plans for *you*. Indeed, I was not, until then, aware that your mind had received that impression which now forms my most anxious hope and desire concerning you. For while I never would or could give encouragement to prospects of the ministry, unless I thought I discovered decided leadings and leanings of mind towards it; so I can truly say, that my first wish for each of my sons in succession has been, from their cradles, that God might fit them for that arduous, responsible, and eminent station, a minister of the gospel of Christ, in deed and in truth. The coincidence of your making your wish known to me at the very period when the lamp of life and hope began to fade, as it concerned your brother, and his subsequent decease, struck me as indicative of God's will respecting you. From that time I have encouraged the prospect, and neglected nothing intentionally which might further your education for that sacred office; ever at the same time watching attentively your general disposition towards Christian experience, knowledge, and conduct. For a man must first be *a true Christian* before he can be *a true minister*. It was with this view that I requested Mr. A. to give you a weekly religious exercise.

From the day that a youth, on Christian principles, is devoted to the ministry, he ought to become a *divinity* student, and all his studies should bend to the one grand object. However valuable in their proper place and connection, yet independently of that connection, classical, mathematical, philosophical, moral, logical studies, and belles-lettres, and literature, all sink to nothing, and only wean the mind from God and Christ. When the *heart* is right in divine matters, then all other things, will become so likewise. The next thing to be considered in your case, was the usual connection between the clerical office and a university residence and degree. This has presented a twofold difficulty to my consideration. The first is, the doubt and fear, lest the atmosphere of a college life, so unpropitious, alike in its gay and its literary habits, to the formation and growth of Christian piety, might endanger the simplicity and stability of your Christian character. This is, however, in a measure overruled by the hope connected with the influence of good Mr. S——'s ministry, and the number of serious young men, from amongst whom, and amongst whom alone, I trust, a few confidential and profitable intimates would be chosen. Nothing would induce me to send you to college, if I did not rely on your maintaining, both outwardly and inwardly, a decidedly Christian walk and profession, regardless alike of the sneers of the scoffer, and the dissipating influence of undecided, however agreeable, companions. It should be observed, that my name stands in a peculiar and somewhat conspicuous point of view; and my son's name would be in several ways connected with the publicity of his father's character. On these subjects I should endeavor to give you hereafter more detailed advice, if you were to become a collegian. In that case I must commit you to the grace of God, and pray for you night and day to be preserved blameless and pure. The second difficulty connected with a college education has been its expense.

\*     \*     \*     \*     \*

Remember, that your religious attainments are my first object, your literary my second. May both go safely hand in hand together.

\*    \*    \*    \*    \*

And now, take my blessing. You are three sons in one to me. Accept a triple blessing, and may the great *Three in One* confirm it. Your welfare lies very close to my heart—your prospects in the ministry, if your life be spared, affect me greatly. I would far sooner hear you preach a gospel sermon from your heart, and visit the bedside of a sick parishioner with the language of experimental consolation, than see you senior wrangler and medallist, with a cold heart and unconverted soul. Think not that I undervalue useful or ornamental literature; for although I regret the monopoly of time and labor, which an artificial and very partial sort of literary acquirements occasion, in our collegiate courses; and while I still more regret the neglect of a theological and religious education, as so prominent a blot in our university plans; yet I wish every clergyman to be a well-informed man, having a mind stored with useful literature, every particle of which should be consecrated to the study of the Bible and the souls of men. It is a great comfort that, notwithstanding the paralyzing influence of sensuality and idleness on the one hand, and of mere human learning and books on the other, God has a chosen people in the university, who are walking in the narrow way that leads to eternal life. If you should go to college, may you ever be found with such, and not with those who bring their fathers' grey hairs with sorrow to the grave; for such would soon be my lot, if you, my loved son, were to fall away from the earnest hopes which I have formed concerning you. Be much in prayer—constantly study your Bible. Read daily some experimental and devotional books. Converse occasionally on the care and conduct of the soul. Remember the *poor* Christians, and when you can, visit and converse with them, as C. does. This is the true school of divinity. It was mine before you; may it be yours after me.

Here close the beautiful and instructive letters of this devoted and faithful father; but the following meditation, written a little previous to his death, furnishes another evidence of the deep and tender solicitude which he ever cherished for his beloved children.

I am this day staying at home during divine service in the afternoon, owing to a cold—Mr. Ayre being here to assist me. The last Sunday afternoon on which I was similarly detained, was in December, 1824, with my dear Wilberforce; he was then within a few weeks of his decease. This day twelvemonth was the day preceding his death.

Dear, blessed boy; in the midst of our daily domestic cheerfulness of spirits, how my heart moans and mourns in tenderest recollections. I see the dear child in all his debilities of body; I hear him speak; I retrace the look of his eye; I hang upon his spiritual language—his affectionate expressions—his devotedness to God—his faithful admonitions—his languid frame—his sweet countenance—his willingness to die.

I lament my own want of more feeling; and yet I feel much. O blessed God, help me, strengthen me, save me. Make his death to be a source of life to me, through the death of Christ—sanctifying his memory to my soul. I want to see more deep and solemn seriousness amongst my children at this time; and yet I know they are not deficient in much good feeling on this subject. Lord, help, bless, and save them also.

My Nugent, too, is since gone—or rather, I have since heard it; for he died some months before his brother, little as we apprehended it when Wilberforce was so beautifully speaking about him, a few days previous to his own death.

Oh, my dear boys, your memorials are most dear to my soul.

I tremble when I think how poorly I have profited by these parental warnings; yet I take some encouragement from the feelings which I am conscious I retain. Lord, increase their influence. In the midst of life I am in death. Who may be taken away next? I sometimes have fearful forebodings—I look around my beloved little circle, and sigh. I check these feelings again, and am ashamed of my weakness. Lord, make Christ to be every thing to me—and then all will, all *must* be well. Oh, keep my Fanny in a serious frame. Let her not forget her past impressions. Bless my Henry, and preserve him in a steady mind, untainted by levities. Cherish my poor Legh, and let not my good hopes concerning him be blighted. Bless the little ones, and make them thine own for ever.

Pardon my weakness, O God, and bless this whole meditation to my own soul.

L. R.

Turvey, Sunday, January 15, 1827.

## Chapter 5

### THE LAST DAYS OF REV. LEGH RICHMOND, IN A LETTER FROM HIS DAUGHTER FANNY

MY DEAR MRS. F——, You wish me to give you an account of the closing scene of my beloved parent's life. This will be attended with some difficulty; for though I was his friend as well as his child, and the endeared companion of his retired hours—and though many events and conversations, full of deep and affecting interest, are indelibly engraved on my memory, yet, as I did not anticipate the mournful bereavement, and omitted to make memoranda at the time, I find now, that much of the detail is irrevocably lost, and I should be afraid to write any thing which was not strictly and literally true.

Yet the recollection of hours spent in my beloved father's study, which was indeed a hallowed sanctuary of devotion, keeps alive in my mind an abiding conviction of the reality and happiness of experimental closet religion. When I feel worldly influence stealing on me, and, consequently, religious duties losing their glow of interest, I have but to think of my departed parent, and of past times, and my heart is again warmed, a new energy in the spiritual life seems imparted, and thus my soul does indeed realize that "the memory of the just is blessed."

I cannot express the veneration and love with which he was regarded by every one of his children. With an understanding of the very first order, a mind elegantly refined and polished, and feelings of the most delicate susceptibility, he had a heart overflowing with intense affection towards each of them, which was shown by daily and hourly attentions of the most winning nature; and they found in him not only a counsellor and instructor, but a companion and bosom friend. They clung to him, indeed, with an almost idolatrous fondness. Each of my brothers and sisters will agree with me in the sentiment of dear Wilberforce, (it was one of my brother's remarks, a little before he closed his eyes upon his weeping parent) "when my heart feels too cold to thank God for any thing else, it can thank him for giving me such a father." He was the spiritual as well as the natural father of that dear boy, and, I trust, others of his children are thus bound to him by a tie strong and lasting as eternity itself. Surely the world does not contain a spot of more sweet and uninterrupted domestic happiness than Turvey rectory presented, before death entered that peaceful dwelling. It was ever the first wish of my beloved father, that our *home* should be happy; and he was never so pleased as when we were all sitting around him. Both in our childhood and youth, every innocent pleasure was resorted to, and all his varied attainments brought into exercise to instruct and amuse us. He was the sun of our little system, and from him seemed to be derived the light and glow of domestic happiness. Like the disciple, whose loving spirit I have often thought my dear father's resembled, his motto was, "Little children, love one another"; and he taught this more effectually by sympathy than even by precept. Religion was unfolded to us in its most attractive form. We saw that it was a happy thing to be a Christian. He was exempt from gloom and melancholy, and entered with life and cheerfulness into all our sports.

But we should not have been thus happy in domestic affection, had not our beloved father so carefully trained us in the religion of Jesus Christ. This was his chief concern, his hourly endeavor. He did not talk much with us about religion; but the books, studies, and even amusements to which he directed us, showed that God was in all his thoughts, and that his great aim was to prepare his children for heaven. Religion was practically taught in all he said and did, and recommended to us in his lovely, domestic character, more powerfully than in any other way. He had a thousand winning ways to lead our infant minds to God, and explain to us the love of the Saviour to little children. It was then our first impressions were received; and though for a time they were obscured by youthful vanities, they were never totally erased; he lived to see them, in some instances, ripened into true conversion. It was his custom, when we were very young, to pray with us alone: he used to take us by turns into his study; and memory still recalls the simple language and affecting earnestness with which he pleaded for the conversion of his child. I used to weep because he wept, though I understood and felt little of his meaning; but I saw it was all love, and thus my earliest impression was associated with the idea, that it was *religion* which made him love us so tenderly, and that prayer was an expression of that love. I was led, in this way, to pray for those who were kind to me, as dear papa did.

In conversation, he did not often urge the subject of religion *directly* on our attention, or question us much as to our personal experience of it. He has sometimes regretted this, and called it his infirmity; but I think he adopted a more successful plan. He used to watch over us most cautiously, and express his opinion in writing: we constantly found letters left in our rooms, with directions to think and pray over them. Reproof was always conveyed in this way; and he also took the same method of questioning us on experimental religion, and of beseeching us to become more decided for God. Sometimes he required an answer, but generally his only request was, that we would "spread his letter before the Lord, and think over it."

His reproofs were inexpressibly tender. He was never angry with us; but when we displeased him, he showed it by such a sad and mournful countenance, that it touched us to the very heart, and produced more effect than any punishment could have done, for we saw that it was our dear father who suffered the most. In this way he gained such an ascendency over our affections, that none of his children could feel happy if his smile was withdrawn, and all regarded that smile as a rich reward.

The anniversaries of our birthdays were always seasons of festivity amongst us. We were generally awakened with his congratulations and blessing. "He rose up early in the morning, and offered sacrifice according to the number of them all: thus did he continually."[1] I love to recall those happy days when our dear father, even in our childish sports, was the mainspring of our joys, and the contriver of every amusement. We always found a birthday present for us, often accompanied by an affectionate note.

Though my dear father was naturally playful and lively, his spirits were easily depressed; and they appeared to undergo a considerable change subsequent to the summer of 1824, the period at which Wilberforce's health began to decline. Wilberforce was most tenderly endeared to him; and there was a strong affinity in their characters. He was just beginning to unfold a very fine understanding, and his intellectual attainments were certainly superior for his age. His mind had been cultivated with much care; and the same elegance of taste and delicacy of feeling, so prominent in my father's character, seemed likewise to mark that of his cherished boy. He manifested the same inclination to the studies of natural philosophy; and when the school lessons were finished, they were constantly engaged together in these pursuits. While the other boys were at play, Wilberforce generally occupied himself in reading in the study, and trying experiments, etc. Mineralogy, in particular, was a favorite science with both; and in each instance it beguiled the hours of declining health. Papa used to amuse himself with his minerals, when all his other scientific pursuits failed to interest him: and poor Willy found the same pleasure in this study; for within a few days of his death, he was searching to see how many different kinds of stones might be enumerated. He had never been absent from home, but was brought up under the immediate eye of his parent, and watched with ceaseless care. He was now preparing for college, and sanguine in the hope that he might distinguish himself;

1 Job 1:5.

and his father was looking forward with deep interest to this period.

In the summer of 1824, my brother ruptured a blood-vessel, and began to spit blood. My dear father discovered great anxiety and alarm, though we did not, for a long time, know how deeply he was affected. He afterwards told mamma, that on *that* morning, as he looked on Wilberforce, he felt a shock which seemed to shatter him to the very soul, and from which he never after recovered. He did, indeed, to use his own words, "roll the troublous calamity on God," but nature sunk under the stroke.

In June, 1824, he took a journey to Scotland, to place Wilberforce under the care of Dr. Stewart. I was their companion in that journey, which I have a mournful pleasure in retracing.

It was very pleasant to travel with my father, he had such an exquisite perception of the beauties of nature; and every object of interest was pointed out to us with his own elegant and devotional associations. Often has he wandered on through the fine scenes of Scotland, both by daylight and moonlight, with poor Willy and myself at his side; and we have sat down together on the sea-shore, or by the hedge-side, while he showed us the image of the Deity in the beauty of his works; and whether he was contemplating the simple wild-flower or the resplendent firmament, he would point to the hand of Omnipotence in both. But his enjoyments at this time greatly depended upon his dear boy's being able to participate in them: if Willy drooped, his spirits were gone, and nature lost its power to charm. I think he was gradually declining in his own health, though he did not complain. He was watching the decay of his beloved son, while his own frame was giving way.

We returned home in October, with no material benefit to our dear invalid: and in January, 1825, after a happy and even triumphant experience of the power of religion, my brother breathed his last gentle sigh in the arms of his afflicted father, who had been, in God's hands, his sole teacher, comforter, and supporter. He was ever at the dying pillow of his suffering child, reading, praying, and comforting him, by day and by night. Before us, he appeared composed and tranquil; but in his retired moments, I have heard him give vent to his feelings with strong "crying and tears." I remember, on the evening of Wilberforce's death, after he had yielded to the first burst of grief, he clasped the inanimate form to his heart, laid it down, dried his tears, and collecting us together in the study, he knelt down, and uttered only the language of praise and gratitude. For a little moment he seemed not only to follow, but to realize his child's flight and welcome to the realms of glory. His whole conduct seemed to express, "though I should see His hand lifted to slay me, yet from that same hand will I look for salvation."

He was much comforted, at this time, in his parish, and in his own family. In the parish, there appeared to be a remarkable revival of religion, particularly among the young people. It might be truly said, "there were added to the church *daily* such as should be saved."[1] This dear boy's death appeared to be the life of many souls; and, in my dear father's own language, "they were the spiritual roses, blooming around the grave of his Willy."

At this time, his character as a pastor shone forth most eminently. He was singularly blessed among his flock. His heart was always in his work; but more particularly did he now preach the word, in season and out of season; "reproving, rebuking, exhorting, with all long-suffering and doctrine." An increase of religious inquiry and anxiety among his people, produced a corresponding increase of visiting and teaching on his part. He regularly met a party of his pious poor at a neighboring cottage, on Tuesdays; frequently a different set on Thursdays; and on Sunday nights, after his fatiguing duties in the church, he met those who had been newly awakened to spiritual life. His heart seemed particularly interested in this last little party, which he used to call his *"spiritual nursery."* I have looked at him with astonishment, when he came to us on Sunday nights. Unceasingly occupied, from ten in the morning till ten at night, he met us with his usual cheerfulness, and entered into animated and interesting conversation, as if no fatigue was felt.

1 Acts 2:47.

On Sunday evenings, after the administration of the sacrament, he met the communicants. On these occasions, he was happy in being surrounded by his spiritual children, dearly beloved by him, and, *on the whole*, he could look on them with approbation and confidence, as his "glory and joy." He was earnest in enforcing upon them consistency of character, and uprightness in temporal affairs: anxious that the enemies of true religion should have no cause to blaspheme from the inconsistencies of its professors, but that his people should adorn the doctrine of God their Saviour, and put to silence the ignorance of foolish men; showing, that *the doctrines of grace are the doctrines of holiness.*

But not in his parish alone was the death of his beloved son rendered singularly useful; his heart was yet more comforted by the hope of solid benefit to his own family. The seed which had been sown with many prayers, and watered with many tears, though it had hitherto lain dormant, began at this time to spring up to the consolation of his bereaved heart. With unspeakable tenderness he watched over the signs of religious anxiety in his children, weeping over them and praying for them with the most vehement affection.

It was a few days after Willy's death, that my own mind was in a state of agitating anxiety—thirsting for the knowledge of God and his holiness, yet feeling so ignorant, dark, and helpless, that I knew not where to look for encouragement or assistance. My ignorance was my great burden. I felt as if I never could *understand* religion, and with these feelings I went into the study, where I found my beloved parent in deep meditation. He seemed to perceive at one glance what was the matter. In his engaging manner he took me on his knee, and folding me to his heart, begged me to tell him all I felt. This was the first time I had opened my mind to him on the subject of religion. I tried to tell him my feelings, dwelling particularly on my ignorance and total blindness in spiritual things. With striking humility and condescension, he replied, "Well, my dear child, we will begin religion together. We will set out in the first step, for I have as much need as you to begin all again. We must go to Jesus

Christ to be set right. We will ask to be taught the first lesson in his religion, and wait in the ignorance of babes for his instruction."

In the following winter, my dear father's failing spirits sustained another severe shock. We were expecting every week our eldest brother from India. He left home at the age of fifteen, and eleven years had now elapsed since his father had seen him. Many singular and affecting circumstances had occurred during this interval. He was thrice shipwrecked; and on one occasion, with only a few others, he got safe to shore. In his early youth he had been a source of much sorrow to his parents, but in a far-distant land his heart was turned to the God of his father; and we received the most satisfactory testimonies to his conversion.

My father's sensitive feelings were strained to the highest pitch in expectation of meeting his dear sailor-boy, who was on his return to visit us; and he was preparing to welcome the "son who was lost and is found, was dead and is alive again,"[1] when the mournful tidings of his death reached us.

Both the mind and body of my dear father were shattered by this intelligence. But though suffering most acutely, he was, as in the former bereavement, the comforter and stay of his family; concealing his own feelings to mitigate theirs.

He used to be much at home at this time, communing with his own heart in his chamber in silence; and no doubt it was his fervent and frequent devotion which strengthened and enabled him "to comfort those who were in trouble, by the comfort wherewith he himself was comforted of God."[2]

He had shut himself up for six weeks, and never appeared in public, except on the Sunday; but when he heard of the anxiety of the people to see him, and share the sorrows of their beloved pastor, he desired them to assemble in the school-room; and he went there to meet them. It was evidently too trying and exciting for his weak frame. For some time he could not speak; but when he recovered

---

1 Luke 15:24.
2 2 Corinthians 1:4.

himself, his address was inexpressibly touching, and yet comforting. The people wept with him, and felt his sorrows as their own. He told them that, conscious of their interest in him, and of their anxiety to know his state of mind under this afflicting rod, he had come on purpose to tell them what God could do for the soul that looked to him for help; that they might magnify the Lord with him, and exalt his name together. He said, that while he had been shut up in the solitude of his study, for the last six weeks, in silent communing with God, he had learnt to feel, "it is good for me that I have been afflicted"[1]—that the experience of his soul during that trying season had been, "in the multitude of my thoughts within me, thy comforts have refreshed my soul."[2]

He then expounded the 107[TH] Psalm, with reference to poor Nugent's case; and expressed himself with more than ordinary energy and freedom. He had been tried, but he came forth as gold. His heavenly Father seemed to say to him, "My son, give *me* thine heart";[3] and the answer of his soul was, "There is none upon earth I desire in comparison of thee."[4] While fainting beneath the heavy load of suffering, he tried to say, like his blessed Master, "The cup which my Father hath given me, shall I not drink it?"[5]

He now resumed his usual cottage meetings, and though his constitution was evidently sinking, and he was laboring far beyond his strength, he could not be persuaded to relax or lessen any of his pastoral engagements. We earnestly requested him to retire for a season from his duties; but, contrary to his usual yielding temper, he remained inflexible; adding, either "it does not injure me," or, "I shall suffer more in my mind by giving them up, than in my body by attending to them." The last year of his life he had a constant irritating cough, which finally settled upon his lungs, and was no doubt much increased by such frequent talking and exposure to the night air.

1  Psalm 119:71.
2  Psalm 94:19.
3  Proverbs 23:26.
4  Psalm 73:25.
5  John 18:11.

I was his constant companion in his visits to the cottages; and he often looked so worn and fatigued, and his spirits sometimes so much affected, apparently with thoughts which he did not express, that I have turned away to weep, and felt undefinable sensations of dread, as the idea crossed my mind, that he was meditating on the final separation.

His public discourses at this time were particularly awakening, as well as confirming. While he warned his flock with deep solemnity, "lest any man fail of the grace of God,"[1] he enlarged on the divine promises, the glory of the Saviour, and the blessedness of the redeemed. A poor woman remarked to me, "Your dear papa preaches as if he was near home."

What he was in his family during the two last years of his life, my pen can but faintly describe. Since Nugent's and Willy's death, his affections were more concentrated on those who were left; and he had also a more endearing tie, for he could now look on some of his family as his spiritual children. In conversation and reading, he could find companions in them. Very pleasant is the recollection of the happy and profitable hours spent in my father's study. He used to awake me at six o'clock every morning, and I read to him till breakfast. He was fond of this early hour, and kept up the plan even through the last winter. But it was injurious to him; for when his cough was bad, and his health sinking daily, he would still rise before the servants were up, call me and my brothers, and then light his own fire, that all might be ready for the reading to commence. He made many valuable remarks as we went on. The last winter months, he wished me to read to him the Cripplegate Lectures. Archbishop Leighton, who was a particular favorite with him, was the last author we read together. Sacred is the memory of those hours: his health was declining, but his soul was ripening for glory; and while listening with interest to the deep experience and triumphant victories of these holy men, he was probably anticipating the near approach of that time when he should join their company.

1 Hebrews 12:15.

His mind was often for days peaceful and tranquil. At such times he never spoke of Wilberforce's death but in terms of gratitude and praise for his happy end: but at other times, the vivid remembrance of his bereavements seemed to overwhelm him, and to occasion new conflicts. I have heard his convulsive sobs and his heart-touching prayers, as I sat in the room beneath the study. I remember, on one day in particular, he had been a long time alone, wishing to be undisturbed; and when I went to him, I found him in deep sorrow. Willy's papers were lying before him, and he appeared in great agitation of mind. In what followed, I was struck with the deep *humility* of his feelings. He said, "it was not unmingled grief for Wilberforce which was then uppermost; he knew he was safe in heaven, and that to him death had been victory: but that the thought painfully harassed him—Shall *I* ever meet him in heaven? shall *I* indeed ever get there? Friends try to comfort me, by saying, (as if they took it for granted) that sorrow is unnecessary; for the separation is very short, and we shall soon meet again in heaven. But alas, there is that inward consciousness of sin, and that perplexing conflict, that *I* cannot take it for granted; and the thought is now sinking me in the very dust, Shall I *indeed* meet him in heaven? am I sure eternity will unite us? And I often shudder, and fall down confounded at the possibility that, after all, I may come short, and our separation be eternal."

This was an affecting and important lesson. I saw that the most holy and established Christian is still a sinner, and feels himself such; that however high his spiritual attainments in this life, the flesh still weighs down the spirit. I had heard and seen my dear father so strong in faith, that heaven seemed realized, and victory obtained; and I fancied *he* could never have a doubt of his salvation. But I found that the father in Christ could weep and tremble like the babe, because of the sin that dwelleth in him.

My dear father's cough continued, and he became very thin; and every one remarked how ill he looked. But he appeared not to notice it, and we thought he did not apprehend danger: we have since found that we were mistaken, and that he "always looked on the cough as a summons from above." He abated nothing of his work, and still continued his visits to the poor. It was in the cottage of sorrow, and by the bed of the dying, that my beloved parent's character appeared the brightest. He was the father as well as the minister of his people; and they brought all their difficulties and troubles to him, and ever found in him a tender and judicious adviser. He had particular pleasure in conversing with the pious poor, and said he had learnt some of his best lessons from them; that the religion of the poor in general was more spiritual and sincere than that of the rich; that they lived more simply the life of faith on the Son of God. I have seen my beloved father in public, when the gaze of admiration was fixed on him, and in the private drawing-room I have beheld him the delight and entertainment of the company, and my heart has exulted in him; but it was when smoothing the pillow of poverty and death, that I most loved and venerated him, and discovered the image of that Saviour "who went about doing good."[1]

In the month of February he went to Cambridge for a fortnight, to enter Henry. This was another subject of great anxiety to his mind: he dreaded the temptations of a college life; and expressed, much solicitude lest his dear inexperienced boy should be corrupted, and his religion injured.

When he returned from Cambridge, we thought he looked better. He had been among friends he loved, and he derived great pleasure from his visit, and appeared more cheerful and lively than we had known him for the last two years. He entered into conversation with spirit, and even amused and entertained us in his engaging manner. We spent one week with him in this improved state of health and spirits; but he soon relapsed into his former thoughtful silence. The next week he caught a fresh cold, and his cough returned with greater violence; yet he would have preached on the following Sunday, if his voice had not entirely failed him. I do not

1 Acts 10:38.

think he imagined that he had seen his people for the last time, but that he anticipated a temporary amendment, sufficient to enable him to go amongst them again. But his ministry was closed; and he was to meet them no more till they met at the judgment-seat of Christ.

To prevent increase of cold, he kept entirely to his study, and never came down stairs after that Sunday; yet he read and wrote as usual.

It may seem extraordinary that he never spoke to us on the subject of his death, but those can understand it who knew the exquisite tenderness and susceptibility of his feelings. His *affection* indeed was almost his *affliction*. He could not bear to witness the sorrow which would have filled our hearts in the certain and near prospect of separation. He wished us, I think, to understand his situation and to observe in silence.

There were no violent symptoms to mark the approach of death, but a gradual decay of strength. He sat with us as usual in his study-chair to the very last day—almost to the last hour. I recollect many things which I did not then understand, but which now show me that he was preparing for death: with surprising calmness he set his house in order. He made a catalogue of his principal books, with memoranda how they were to be disposed of; also of his minerals and philosophical apparatus; he emptied all the cupboards round the room, which had not been done for many years; he burnt every book which he thought of an injurious tendency. All this was done for the most part in silence, it being painful for him to speak, even in a whisper. I have seen him sit for an hour together in the deepest abstraction of thought—then he would raise his eyes, the tears streaming down his pale cheeks, clasping his hands, as if in the fervency of importunate prayer—and again all was composure, and he looked peaceful and happy. He seemed to be maintaining a constant communion with God. I know he felt deeply for his children, whom he was about to leave young and inexperienced—exposed to a world of sin and temptation. My brother and I have frequently heard him break forth in prayer for us when we had scarcely closed his door. The sounds were faint and broken, but we understood their import; and the unutterable tenderness of his manner towards us is even now too affecting to dwell upon. He would sometimes open his arms for me to come to him, and laying his head upon my shoulder, would fall again into deep thought. His parish also was always upon his mind. He was continually inquiring about the people, and sending me with messages to them; and he listened with much interest to the report I made of them.

One of his converts, a young girl of nineteen, was at this time on the bed of death, and my dear father regretted much he could not visit her; but he was very anxious to comfort and instruct her through me. She survived him two months, and died in the same peace, perhaps with more triumph. She said, just before her death, "she longed yet more for heaven, because her dear minister was there to welcome her." I know that he was full of anxiety for a suitable successor, and the idea of his flock being dispersed hung heavy upon his spirits. One morning, when I was sitting near him, he burst into tears, and said, "Oh, my parish, my poor parish; I feel as if I had done nothing for it, as if it had been so much neglected. I have not done half that I ought." It was more than I could bear to hear him speak in this way; for I had seen him in weariness, and painfulness, and watching, spending and being spent, if by any means he might win souls to Christ. I suggested to him his labors, and the singular usefulness of his ministry, especially within the last two years; he would still reply, "No thanks to me, no thanks to me. I see it so different now, as if I had done just nothing. I see nothing but neglect, and duties left undone." I could not help reflecting on the different aspect things must have when eternity is opening upon us.

He was considerably cheered soon after this, by the prospect of Mr. H—— becoming his curate; it seemed to revive him; he lost sight of other troubles in the thought that his church would be well supplied.

He often recurred to Henry's residence at college, and talked of his fears for his dear boy till he was quite spent. He would say, "I have seen the ruin of so many promising youths by a college life, and those apparently as amiable and pious as my own dear child. I know the difficulty of maintaining spiritual religion at Cambridge. Even studies which are in themselves lawful, and which he ought to pursue, have a tendency to weaken piety, and interrupt private devotion. *Christ has often been crucified between classics and mathematics.* I wish him to be diligent in his studies, but the Bible is the proper library for a young man entering into the church. If he does but understand the Bible experimentally, I shall be content. Bid him, Fanny, to be very careful of his companions, that they be few, and more advanced in religion than himself; and particularly that he attends Mr. Simeon's ministry. It cheers my heart, that there is such a ministry at Cambridge. Be sure you talk to him about these things. Warn him of declensions, and against sacrificing religion to the desire of distinction. That dear boy, and his approaching trials, are never out of my thoughts; I think of him by day, and dream of him by night."

We found in his desk a sheet of paper, on which was written "Cambridge documents." These were directions for Henry, but not finished. He had often expressed a great desire to see a son in the church, ready to take his place. "If I might but hear a true gospel sermon from one of my children, I should die in peace." On another occasion, he expressed great delight that his young friend C—— H—— visited the poor, and said, "you must recommend this to Henry, as the very best preparation for the ministry. Try, my dear Fanny, to keep him up to it. Tell him his poor father learnt his most valuable lessons for the ministry, and his most useful experience in religion, in the poor man's cottage."

The last time he spoke to me on personal religion, he endeavored to establish my mind in the doctrine of assurance, and enlarged on its importance, and its tendency to promote both comfort and obedience. He pointed to Archbishop Leighton as my pattern: "See how holily and lovingly that man walked with God, because he believed that his salvation was safe and settled, that he was chosen in Christ. Try, my dear child, to expand your views; look at the magnificent scheme of salvation—the contract between the Father and his eternal Son. How much better to look out of self, and see all perfected in Christ. You will never be happy and strong, till you grasp the covenant plan of redemption. You live upon self too much: you will get misery and despair, but nothing else, by looking to yourself. Live upon Christ; he has done all for you, if you could but believe it."

Of the last sermons I read to him, one was entitled, "Hope amidst Billows"; the other, "The Believer a Hero." This last I read twice to him; and he expressed much delight in listening to it. It seemed to suit the state of his mind, and corresponded with his own sentiments. At one part of the sermon he stopped me, that he might meditate on what he heard, and then he said, "Read it again." It seemed to cheer his mind. When I had finished it, "This," said he, "exactly expresses what I would say to you; that is just my sentiment"; and he told me to turn down the leaf, that he might show it to mamma. I have copied the passage; it appears to me very beautiful, and is greatly endeared to me, as having comforted my dear father a few days only before his death.

"The fear of God is not a perplexing doubting, and distrust of his love: on the contrary, it is a fixed resting and trust in his love. Many who have some truth of grace,[1] are, through weakness, filled with disquieting fears; but possibly, though they perceive it not, it may be in some a point of wilfulness, a little latent undiscerned affectation of scrupling and doubting, placing much of religion in it. True, where the soul is really solicitous about its interest in God, that argues some grace; but being vexingly anxious about it, argues that grace is weak and low. A spark there is, even discovered by that smoke; but the great smoke still continuing, and nothing seen but it, argues there is little fire, little faith, little love. And this, as it is unpleasant to thyself, so it is to God, as smoke to the eyes. What if

---

1 This is the expression used in the original. It is equivalent to saying, "Many who are not without a measure of true grace," etc. (*Original footnote*)

one should be always questioning with a friend, whether he loved him or not, and upon every little occasion were ready to think he doth not, how would they disrelish their society together, though truly loving each other. The far more excellent way, and more pleasing both to ourselves and to God, were to resolve on humble trust, reverence, and confidence, being most afraid to offend, delighting to walk in his ways, loving him and his will in all; and then resting persuaded of his love, though he chastise us. And even though we offend him, and see our offenses in our chastisements, yet he is good, plenteous in redemption, ready to forgive; therefore let Israel hope and trust. Let my soul roll itself on him, and adventure there all its weight. He bears greater matters, upholding the frame of heaven and earth, and is not troubled nor burdened with it."

Three days after, he asked me to read one of Newton's letters, from the volume entitled, "The Aged Pilgrim's Triumph." He listened to me with interest, but did not speak, except to thank me.

When his meals were brought to him, he used to clasp his wasted hands, and ask a blessing. "I thank thee, heavenly Father, for these undeserved mercies to such an unworthy sinner." There may be nothing more in the words than any other Christian would utter; but the humility and reverence of his manner deeply affected us. . . .

He had a great dislike to keep his bed; and I cannot but acknowledge the goodness of God, that it was not necessary. He rose every day, to the last, and sat as usual in his study; only getting up a little later, and going to bed earlier, as his strength gradually failed him. The last fortnight he was very silent, and appeared constantly in prayer and meditation—waiting his dismissal, and the end of his earthly pilgrimage. At this time, nothing seemed to disturb him; and he appeared to realize the full import of that blessed promise, "Thou wilt keep him in perfect peace, whose mind is stayed on thee."[1] I have often thought he exemplified the faith his favorite Leighton commends: "Let thy soul roll itself on God, and adventure there all its weight." It was indeed an unspeakable delight to us to

1 Isaiah 26:3.

observe the unruffled calm of his soul; and it confirmed our minds in the truth and value of the doctrines he had taught for thirty years. We had seen our beloved father prostrate in soul before God, under a consciousness of indwelling sin; we had heard him bemoaning himself, after a long life of usefulness, as an unprofitable servant, renouncing again and again all hope of salvation by his own goodness, and fleeing to Jesus as his only refuge. To use his words to C—— H——, "It is only by coming Christ as a little child, and as for the first time, that I can get peace." Yet, though for a time perplexed, he was not forsaken. We saw him comforted of God, and proving what he had often said to me, "Christ has firm hold of you, however feeble your grasp of him": and now we saw him strong in faith, and in the last hour of dissolving nature, rejoice in the sure and certain hope of the glory of God. He did indeed find, to use the dying words of my beloved brother, "the rest that Christ gives is sweet." He was silent, but it was a most expressive silence, and revealed emotions of joy and praise not to be described. Many touching circumstances occurred, which showed both the man and the Christian; but they are of too delicate a nature to be communicated beyond the circle of his own family.

Two days before his death, he received a letter, mentioning the conversion of two persons, one of whom was a clergyman, by the perusal of his Tract, "The Dairyman's Daughter." When the letter was given him, he seemed too feeble to open it himself, and desired Henry to read it to him. The contents deeply interested him. He raised himself in his chair, lifted up his hand, and then let it fall down again, while he repeatedly shook his head. His manner spoke the greatest humility, as if he would say, "How unworthy of such honor!" For a few minutes it seemed to administer a cordial to his fainting spirit, and led our minds, in reference to our dear father, to contemplate the near fulfilment of that promise, "They that turn many to righteousness, shall shine as the stars for ever and ever."[1]

On Tuesday, the 8TH of May, he rose later than usual: I think it

1 Daniel 12:3.

was twelve before he got into the study; and he was so weak, that he had great difficulty in walking there from his bedroom. His breath was short, and he looked very pale, but he said he felt no pain. He sat on his reading-chair, with his head resting on a pillow: his countenance and manner was calm and peaceful. In the afternoon he could scarcely support himself; and I kneeled on a chair behind him, and he laid his head on my shoulder. Once he seemed to be fainting, but he soon revived, and, looking calmly at me, he said, "Better now, love."

Mamma could no longer stay in the room, and I was left alone with him till five. He still said nothing, except to assure me he felt no pain. To the very last, it appeared to be his great desire to spare our feelings. We now persuaded him to go to bed, but we little thought death was so near. He could not walk, and we were going to ring for a servant to assist him; but he said, "I should like *Henry* to carry me." He was wasted to a skeleton: Henry took him up with great ease, and we all followed. I shall never forget this most affecting moment: it was a moment of anguish to me, more than the last scene. He seemed to know that he was leaving the study, never to return to it: his look told me that he knew it. This was his favorite room, where for more than twenty years he had constantly carried on his pursuits. There he had written his books—studied his sermons—instructed his children—conversed with his flock, and offered daily sacrifice of praise and prayer. I watched him, as Henry carried him out: his countenance preserved the same look of fixed composure. He raised his head, and gave one searching look round the room, on his books—his table—his chair—his wife—his children— and then the door closed on him for ever. He gave the same look round the gallery, through which we passed, as if he was bidding farewell to every thing. There was a peculiar expression in his countenance, which I cannot describe: it seemed to say, "Behold, I die, but God will be with you." Henry seated him in a chair, and he sat to be undressed, like a little dependent child, in deep silence, but without the ruffling of a feature.

About nine, he seemed rather wandering, and made an effort to speak, but we could not make out his meaning; only we perceived he was thinking of his church, for we heard him say several times, "It will be all confusion." Mamma asked him what would be confusion. "The church. There will be such confusion in my church."

About ten o'clock, he signified to mamma, in the gentlest whisper, that he wished to be left alone—to send us all away, and draw the curtains round him.

About half past ten, Mrs. G——, the kind and faithful nurse of Willy, tapped at my door. I was reading the Bible, and had just reached that verse, "That ye be not slothful, but followers of them who through faith and patience inherit the promises."[1] I have thought the coincidence remarkable; at least, I trust it will ever give a quickening influence to that passage, when I read it. She told me to come and look at my father. She said, she could hardly tell whether there was any change or not. I hurried to him. He raised his eyes to heaven, and then closed them. I put my cheek upon his; and I believe at that instant I felt, for I could not hear, his dying sigh. I thought he was sleeping, and continued looking at him, till Hannah said, "Your dear papa is in heaven." I did not think him dead, and I rubbed his still warm hands, and kissed his pale cheek, and entreated him to speak one word to me: but I soon found it was the silence of death. All turned to poor mamma, who was insensible; and I was thus left alone with my dear father, kneeling beside him with his hand in mine. The same holy calm sat on his countenance, and seemed to say, "Thanks be to God, who hath given me the victory."[2]

The scene that followed was truly afflictive. The grief of the widow and the fatherless was unchecked; for he who had always comforted them, and bid them kiss the rod, was no longer with them. The *contrast* between the after-scene of Wilberforce's and our beloved parent's death was peculiarly affecting to me. When my

---

1  Hebrews 6:12.

2  1 Corinthians 15:57.

brother died, my father assembled us together, to implore resignation, and offer praise. But when he himself departed, all seemed gone. There was no one to collect us; and we were scattered in wild sorrow, with a feeling of desolation which was quite unutterable.

We cannot, we ought not to forget such a father. Yea, I would add, "when I forget thee, may my right hand forget her cunning."[1]

The hand of God has gone out against us; yet "the seed of the righteous is not forsaken."[2] He has cut off the "stream which made us glad"; but praised be his name, he invites us to the "living fountain," where our souls may drink and be satisfied.

Believe me, my dear Mrs. F.,

Your very affectionate,

F. R.

---

1 Psalm 137:5.
2 See Psalm 37:25.

Made in the USA
Columbia, SC
16 December 2023

28653656R00083